The Special Mission
of Grandparents

THE SPECIAL MISSION
OF GRANDPARENTS

Hearing, Seeing, Telling

C. Margaret Hall

BERGIN & GARVEY
Westport, Connecticut • London

Library of Congress Cataloging-in-Publication Data

Hall, C. Margaret (Constance Margaret)
  The special mission of grandparents : hearing, seeing, telling /
  C. Margaret Hall.
      p.   cm.
    Includes bibliographical references and index.
    ISBN 0–89789–672–6 (alk. paper)
    1. Grandparenting.   2. Grandparents.   I. Title.
  HQ759.9.H34   1999
  306.874′5—dc21   99–12701

British Library Cataloguing in Publication Data is available.

Library of Congress Catalog Card Number: 99–12701
ISBN: 0–89789–672–6

First published in 1999

Bergin & Garvey, 88 Post Road West, Westport, CT 06881
An imprint of Greenwood Publishing Group, Inc.
www.greenwood.com

Printed in the United States of America

∞™

The paper used in this book complies with the
Permanent Paper Standard issued by the National
Information Standards Organization (Z39.48–1984).

10 9 8 7 6 5 4 3 2 1

Contents

I

STARTING POINTS

1

Becoming a Grandparent

Becoming a grandparent is often scary. Perhaps this new status signals the onset of old age, or becoming one of a few remaining elders in a young family. However, although there are not many social rituals in today's society to ease the transition from parent to grandparent, well-wishers frequently abound, and greeting cards may be sent to mark the occasion.

To some extent the younger you are when you become a grandparent—especially if you are thirty or forty years of age—the more you will be expected to pitch in and share parenting chores and responsibilities. In families where difficult circumstances must be combatted, grandparents may in fact have to raise their grandchildren in place of the parents. Having children or grandchildren early in life is frequently thought of as a personal and social crisis in modern industrial societies, especially when mothers are poor, unmarried, and without extensive family support.

Strong families, as well as dysfunctional or fragmented families, are found in all social classes, races, and ethnic groups. Although in significant ways becoming a grandparent is experienced differently within different social classes, races, ethnic groups, and genders, there are also important similarities in how patterns of family interaction get shifted and stressed when a new birth occurs. *The Special Mission of Grandparents:*

Hearing, Seeing, Telling describes some of these most significant similarities in becoming a grandparent and in participating
in families and communities.

When we take a look at what goes on among grandparents of
all social classes, races, and ethnic groups, at least on the surface
of things it appears that all goes well. Talk in grandparent city is
typically sweetened with superlatives about enjoying grandchildren and taking pride in grandchildren's accomplishments, and
there do not seem to be many complaints. Is this enough, however? Is this what life is all about?

When we listen more closely to grandparents' conversations
about specific aspects of grandparenting, or particular grandparenting experiences, we find clues to suggest that family
stresses and tensions mar some grandparenting pleasures and
satisfactions. Stephanie, Rasheed, Maria, and Carlos all have
such concerns and discomfort about their grandparenting
situations, which will be discussed later in this chapter.

This book shows grandparents how to deal with family issues
that limit their fulfillment as grandparents and suggests a range
of constructive and effective ways to grandparent. It also motivates grandparents to participate more fully in different kinds of
family exchanges between generations and to work towards improving conditions for personal and social development in communities as well as families.

In order to accomplish these goals, we first need to examine
how we become grandparents and how the initial stages of becoming a grandparent frequently set the tone for future grandparenting behavior. Because similar problems and dilemmas
related to becoming a grandparent exist in vastly different families, looking at some of the relationship tensions of Stephanie,
Rasheed, Maria, and Carlos helps us to understand our own
family situations as well as theirs.

Stephanie, a sixty-year-old grandmother of three, makes her
joy and anguish in being a grandparent known to her friends. "I
long for my grandchildren to visit! It is impossible for me to

travel to see them, so I just hope that sooner or later they will come to see me," she says wistfully.

Rasheed has another concern. "I wish I got along with my son's wife better. I always feel to be in the way when I drop by to see my grandson." Rasheed is a fifty-five-year-old grandfather who lives a few blocks away from his son and his family.

Things are going well enough for Maria and Carlos at present, but they sense that this state of affairs is precarious. "We do everything we can for our granddaughters," says Maria. "Carlos gives them money, I cook for them and buy them gifts, and we take them with us whenever we go to the beach, but," she sighs, "we're afraid that when they get older—which will be soon—they will prefer to spend time with their friends rather than with us." Maria and Carlos immigrated to the United States more than twenty years ago, and they live about twelve miles from their two granddaughters.

When we know more about Stephanie, Rasheed, Maria, and Carlos we can begin to assess whether their concerns are realistic. As we consider their particular circumstances, however, we should also bear in mind some basic issues about grandparenting, so that we can understand more fully what options grandparents have. We need to answer questions such as: To what extent is grandparenting a process that begins at the time we were born? Does becoming a grandparent inevitably bring with it certain hazards? Can Stephanie, Rasheed, Maria, and Carlos do something to feel more secure and more effective as grandparents? What do you think the outcome will be in these situations?

In examining Stephanie's circumstances more closely, we learn that she is an able-bodied woman who owns a car and works full-time as a legal secretary. Stephanie is well paid and lives modestly in her own house. She was divorced after she had been married for five years, and she dotes on the son and daughter she raised more or less single-handedly. Stephanie made many sacrifices for her son and daughter over the years, and she is convinced that she did a good job as a single parent. She thinks that it is her children's turn to make sacrifices now and that she is entitled to have her grandchildren visit her in her home on a regular basis.

Stephanie makes no consistent efforts to visit her children and grandchildren herself. She has fixed ideas about child care, and she assumes that her children will arrange for her grandchildren to visit her on her terms. Even though she is surprised that her children do not come to see her more often, she reassures herself that this is because her grandchildren are still young and that very soon she will have opportunities to spend more time with them.

For his part, Rasheed is afraid to provoke his daughter-in-law's anger. This fear stops him from visiting his grandson frequently, in spite of the fact that he lives close by and is very fond of his son. Instead of becoming more considerate and more careful about making the time he spends with his grandson also meet his daughter-in-law's needs, he clings to his belief that he should be able to visit his grandson whenever he wants.

Rasheed is unwilling to work out his differences with his daughter-in-law directly, and he resents her attempts to protect her privacy. Rasheed expects his daughter-in-law to accommodate his wishes because he is a grandfather, even though he realizes that this emotional issue blocks his access to his grandson. Rasheed voices his frustration about the conflict to his son, but his son feels unable to put things right by persuading his wife to do things the way his father wants. Rasheed does not know how to get through this impasse.

Both Maria and Carlos are convinced that they are wonderful grandparents. They have had modest financial successes since they immigrated to the United States over twenty years ago, and they are justifiably proud of their many accomplishments. Consequently, their grandparenting consists largely of giving material goods and services to their children and their families.

So far Maria and Carlos have gained their granddaughters' love and attention through their gifts and shared activities.

However, neither Maria nor Carlos feels that this closeness with their granddaughters will stand the test of time. They fear that they will lose their granddaughters to friends and competing interests as their granddaughters mature. Furthermore, even though Maria and Carlos sense that their current status as much-loved grandparents is threatened, they do not know what to do. Given their doubts and confusion, they decide that the safest course of action is to continue to provide goods and services to their granddaughters as before.

Like Stephanie, Rasheed, Maria, and Carlos, many grandparents in today's society are bewildered and perplexed about how they can play significant roles in their families. They remember, or they remember learning, that grandparents were influential in families in bygone days or that grandparents still wield power in families in far-off places. Consequently, they wonder whether the past, or life at the other end of the world, is a kind of golden age where they would count for much more than today's circumstances in the United States seem to allow. They also wonder, by contrast, if it could be a kind of social progress to have grandparents play relatively unimportant roles in modern families, because they know that some loosening of grandparenting responsibilities can feel like personal freedom and independence. However, even though many grandparents realize that contemporary families can often survive fairly well without any contributions from grandparents, they do not believe that this is the best of all worlds.

The Special Mission of Grandparents shows that in spite of grandparents' diminished social status in current times, grandparents who deepen their understanding of their possibilities and opportunities can become effective both as grandparents and as members of communities. This volume details how specific deliberate moves increase the impact grandparents have in

their families and in society, so that grandchildren and others
benefit from their actions and purposeful interventions.

In considering the overall characteristics of grandparents'
roles in today's industrial societies, we need to remember that a
hidden reality makes grandparents particularly able to contribute constructively to their families and communities. Grandparents are uniquely rooted in both the past and present
generations of their families, and this broad base of connectedness gives them a distinctly advantageous operating position.
Their strategic intergenerational relatedness enables them to
have an enduring influence on their grandchildren and future
generations.

The Special Mission of Grandparents points out ways for
grandparents to cut through their role confusion and ambiva-
lence and suggests how to take strategic action in their families
and communities. Thus this book encourages grandparents to
work systematically towards increasing the welfare of their
grandchildren, families, future generations, and society. Although this is a tall order, it is a realistic and creative lifetime
challenge, which brings meaning and enjoyment to grandparents, grandchildren, and others.

IN THE BEGINNING

Much of what we do as grandparents grows out of our earliest impressions of our families, and particularly out of our experiences of our own grandparents. Knowing some of the ways in
which families influence the grandparents we become starts
with childhood recollections of grandparents. Understanding
flows from reflecting on cherished memories of grandparents;
on how we may have suffered because of our grandparents, or
from not having grandparents; on whether our fathers' or our
mothers' parents were more influential in our upbringing; on
why one set of grandparents or one grandparent had a particu-

larly strong impact on us; and on how we wish our grandparents had been different.

These memories, impressions, and thoughts are vital starting points for becoming a special mission grandparent. Unless our ideas about becoming a grandparent are deliberately forged, we automatically repeat or react to how we believe we were grand-parented and parented. Optimally we should choose to grand-parent in some of the same ways that we choose to do other things we care about. We can be just as creative, strong, and imaginative in our grandparenting as we are in our work and lei-sure activities.

Considering Stephanie, Rasheed, Maria, and Carlos shows us how their childhood experiences of their grandparents influ-ence the assumptions and expectations they have about becom-ing grandparents. Furthermore, it is only when Stephanie, Rasheed, Maria, and Carlos became aware of the strength of these family influences that they began to neutralize them and were sufficiently free to grandparent as they chose.

Stephanie had very meaningful relationships with all her grandparents. She lived fairly close to both sets of grandparents as a child, and her parents took her and her brother to visit them on a regular, alternating basis. This meant that Stephanie saw one or the other pair of grandparents most weekends until she was a teenager, and because of these continuities she took her grandparents for granted. They were integral parts of her early family experiences.

Rasheed had a close relationship with one pair of his grand-parents. He lived on the same block as his father's parents when he was a boy, and these grandparents stopped by to see him at least once or twice a week. Rasheed's mother was extremely fond of her mother-in-law, and Rasheed's visits with his grand-parents often included overnight stays at his home or theirs. Rasheed's father's parents and his own parents were almost in-terchangeable in his mind and affections when he was a child.

By contrast, neither Maria nor Carlos had close relationships with their grandparents. They were both raised in very poor families in El Salvador. Maria's and Carlos's parents left the villages where they had been born soon after their marriages, and they settled in the same fairly distant city. Because travel back to their villages of origin was difficult and costly, Carlos and Maria did not have frequent ongoing contacts with their grandparents while they were growing up. Furthermore, because their grandparents were so poor, Carlos's and Maria's parents supported them financially until their grandparents died at fairly young ages.

COMMITMENT

Another significant aspect that influences the kind of grandparents people become is the type of commitment they make to this role. The media have long raised questions about the difficulties people have in making commitments to personal relationships and families, but these debates usually revolve around marital bonds or parental responsibilities rather than grandparenting. However, grandparents differ widely in the degrees of commitment they make to being grandparents. Furthermore, some grandparents essentially give up grandparenting responsibilities before they begin, because they do not know what it was like to be grandparented or even parented.

Whatever our past circumstances have been, the commitments we make to become strong grandparents can override problems with grandparents and parents, as long as our understanding of the possibilities and realities of grandparenting is sound. Having a clearly defined vision and attainable ideals about grandparenting helps grandparents to become effective agents of change. This book shows grandparents how to practice principles in their everyday lives that actualize their grandparenting ideals.

Some of the opportunities and beneficial consequences from assuming a special mission as grandparents can be seen through a longer-range view of Stephanie, Rasheed, Maria, Carlos, and their families. Although each person interprets the special mission of grandparents differently, the individual behavior as a special mission grandparent eventually establishes new but similar patterns of exchanges with other family members.

When Stephanie understood that she needed to play a more active role as a grandmother, she started to let go of many of her preprogrammed assumptions about what she thought of as her grandmother entitlements. She planned visits to her grandchildren according to her adult children's and grandchildren's needs, and she undertook these trips on a regular basis. As a result of increasing the number and quality of her contacts with her children's families, other relationships in Stephanie's family also changed. Her family's bonds became more flexible, and she was able to accomplish her preferred goals with her grandchildren.

It took Rasheed a longer time to realize that his daughter-in-law wished him well and welcomed his interest in her son, as long as he was considerate in the timing and frequency of his visits. He eventually discovered that when he gave his daughter-in-law advance notice of his wish to drop by to see his grandson, he gained freer access to him. As a result, Rasheed not only visited his grandson more frequently, but he also took him on more outings. His cooperation with his daughter-in-law built trust between them, and Rasheed became closer to his son as well as to his daughter-in-law and grandson.

Although Maria and Carlos continued to give gifts to their granddaughters, they also strengthened their bonds with them through deliberately initiating personal, meaningful conversations. Maria and Carlos recounted their clearest memories of their childhoods to their granddaughters, and in doing so they bridged the emotional estrangement they had felt between the first half of their lives in El Salvador and their current circumstances in the United States. Coming full circle in this way drew their granddaughters into their families' shared past and gave them all a more secure emotional foundation for moving into the future.

Understanding something about the lives of Stephanie, Rasheed, Maria, and Carlos scratches the surface of what it means to come to grips with major grandparenting issues. None of us has exactly the same difficulties to deal with as Stephanie, Rasheed, Maria, and Carlos, but we may face similar challenges. Because families interact as systems or networks, it is important to know where we stand in relation to other family members, whether we are grandparents or not. However, the strategic intergenerational position of grandparents suggests the particular importance of making a commitment, as a grandparent, to work towards increasing opportunities for the growth and development of self and others.

When we look at Stephanie, Rasheed, Maria, and Carlos in their roles of becoming and being grandparents, specific questions help us to gain a fuller understanding of how they defined their special mission as grandparents. We need to ask ourselves, Which practices worked best for Stephanie, Rasheed, Maria, and Carlos in becoming special mission grandparents? How can these strategies be incorporated in everyday life so that they benefit grandchildren and other family members? How can grandparents best make effective family and community contributions?

The following chapters spell out particular approaches and techniques that help grandparents to achieve their most constructive goals, as well as show grandparents how to apply these strategies on a daily basis. This book also describes how hearing, seeing, and telling can be significant means to strengthen relationships between grandparents and grandchildren and among family members.

Even at an early stage of making grandparenting commitments and goals, Stephanie, Rasheed, Maria, and Carlos changed their relationships with their grandchildren and increased the meaningfulness of their exchanges with relatives in different generations. They became more effective grandparents because they chose to believe that they have purpose and direction as grandparents and that what they do can increase their families' well-being. Furthermore, because Stephanie, Rasheed, Maria, and Carlos expressed their grandparenting ideals through plans, strategies, and actions, they had a beneficial impact on an increasing number of family members through time.

The Special Mission of Grandparents invites readers to go beyond understanding some of the family origins of grandparenting to discover ways to open up families and communities, so that there are more growth-enhancing conditions and opportunities for grandchildren, relatives, and future generations. This volume describes effective ways to grandparent, and how aware grandparents can contribute to society as well as to their families.

2

The Special Mission of Grandparents

Grandparenting often feels foisted upon us rather than chosen. Grandparents' different circumstances evoke contrasting reactions: they may not approve of their children's mates; they may want their children to marry later, or to avoid marriage; they may disapprove of unmarried liaisons, especially when their grandchildren are born from these unions; they may believe that grandchildren block career opportunities for their daughters and sons; they may be deliriously happy to be grandparents; or they may long for grandchildren they do not yet have.

Although you can definitely choose to accept or reject grandparenting responsibilities, the decision to have grandchildren is beyond your control. This book invites you to embrace the opportunity to be a grandparent when it presents itself and to make worthwhile contributions as a grandparent in your family and in society.

The special mission of grandparents calls forth the vocational aspects of being a grandparent. We must also come to terms with some rather personal issues about family responsibilities when we assess what a special mission as a grandparent might mean for us. Do we really want to be active grandparents? To what extent do we respond willingly and positively to grandparenting possibilities through time? If we do not have to raise our grandchildren, are we an intimate part of their lives? Do we make space in our busyness to interact meaningfully with our grandchildren whether they are infants, children, adolescents, or young adults? Do we want to organize our lives around our grandchildren's needs as well as our own? Can we design and pursue grandparenting goals that give meaning, purpose, and direction to our day-to-day exchanges with grandchildren, relatives, and communities?

Responding to the calling of grandparenthood as a special mission increases our motivation and determination to be effective grandparents and enables us to work towards improving conditions and opportunities for our grandchildren and others. Accepting this mission encourages us to focus on what we really want to accomplish both for and with our grandchildren, as well as what we want to contribute to our families and communities. When we begin to believe in, and to take seriously, our goals as grandparents, we realize that we must first cultivate sufficient access to our grandchildren to be able to lead them towards rich, meaningful fulfillment.

Victor, Ella, Henry, and Sheila seemed to be passive, relatively uninvolved grandparents. Although they managed to keep up with what seemed to be constant rounds of required gift giving and family reunions, they wished that they could get more involved with their grandchildren.

"I don't want to be just another relative to my grandchildren," says Victor. "I think I can be more of a grandparent than this!"

"I'm never happier than when I do things with my grandchildren, but I feel so sad when they don't visit me," is Ella's wistful lament. "When they are here, I don't do much more than try to keep up with them."

"It's hard to remember who wants what when birthdays come around, and I can't spend much time with each grandchild," is Henry's concern. "I want to get to know my grandchildren more than this."

Sheila expresses her bewilderment about grandparenting by her comment, "My attention gets too divided by the sheer number of our grandchildren, as well as their different needs. I must find a way to make more sense out of this complicated situation."

Because Victor had been estranged from his children when they were growing up, they are discomforted by his wish to participate as a grandparent in their families now. By contrast, Ella had been a dedicated mother, even though she had married and divorced twice, each marriage being followed by a lengthy period of single parenting. Currently she meets most of her companionship needs through her grandchildren. Henry and Sheila share a different set of circumstances. Although both of their first marriages had ended in divorce, they have been married to each other for almost twenty-six years. They have several grandchildren from their prior marriages, as well as from their own, and they find it difficult to build satisfying relationships with their large band of grandchildren.

Victor, Ella, Henry, and Sheila began to shape their lives more meaningfully and more independently as soon as they began to believe that they could have a strong positive influence on each of their grandchildren. Victor realizes that he could harm his grandchildren by not relating to them consistently and thoughtfully, but he also really wants to have a constructive impact on their lives. His confidence in his own good intentions allows him to work towards having meaningful relationships with his grandchildren. Ella looks to her special mission as a grandparent to bring more balance into her daily activities. In fact, claiming a special mission as a grandparent motivates her to get involved with her community as well as with her grandchildren. For Henry and Sheila defining their grandparenting objectives includes first deciding which of them will have the closer bond with each of the grandchildren in their complex blended family.

Believing that, as grandparents, we can make a difference in our families and in our communities changes our orientations to everyday life and eventually strengthens our overall contributions to our families and communities. Holding our own and consistently doing what we believe in are vital starting points for changing the ways in which we interact with members of our families and communities. These results occur because gaining improved access to our grandchildren, intensifying our efforts to grandparent effectively, and making more direct contributions to our communities as well as to our families gradually shift entrenched family and community exchanges to be more open, more flexible, and more life-enhancing.

Victor had to repair many broken bridges in his relationships with his children before he could gain adequate access to his grandchildren. He had to neutralize the strong resistance due to his rejection of family responsibilities and absences from family events over the years. Victor's children are particularly resentful of his lack of interest in their welfare when they were young, and they are understandably wary about letting him see his grandchildren on a regular basis. Even though Victor's children realize that his current wish to be involved with his grandchildren is his way of saying that he regrets the past, this is not enough to convince them that sooner or later he would not hurt his grandchildren emotionally by turning away from them.

In spite of her two broken marriages and extended single parenting, Ella consistently made parenting her highest priority. However, her world of activities has diminished considerably over the years, and presently she looks to her grandchildren too much to meet her emotional needs. Although she still loves her children as much as ever, her energies are almost entirely caught up in relating to her grandchildren. Therefore, for Ella, beginning to believe in a special mission as a grandparent inspired her to search out opportunities to become active in her community. She realizes that being involved in organizations and issues outside her family will give her a firmer foundation for her own well-being and set a stronger example for her grandchildren.

Henry and Sheila began their special mission as grandparents by deciding which of them will assume responsibility for each of their grandchildren. They agreed that Henry would continue to build strong relationships with his grandchildren from his first marriage; that Sheila would concentrate on bonding with her grandchildren from her first marriage; and that they would share responsibilities for the grandchildren from their own marriage. Rather than trying to be all things to all of their grandchildren, Henry and Sheila found that narrowing the scope of their shared outreach to their grandchildren in their blended family enabled them to give more one-on-one attention to each grandchild. This strategy freed both Sheila and Henry to work towards what they really wanted to achieve with each grandchild, as well as with their communities.

The experiences of Victor, Ella, Henry, and Sheila suggest a variety of ways in which grandparents may think of themselves as having a special mission as a grandparent in their families and communities. Without this goal, grandparents tend not to look sufficiently closely at those aspects of their behavior with their grandchildren, relatives, and communities that they choose and therefore can change. Nor do they usually connect what they do in their communities with their effectiveness as grandparents.

In order to understand what the special mission of grandparents can be, it is useful to think of the possibilities as involving choices about different kinds of contributions. The following list summarizes some of the many options grandparents have.

The special mission of grandparents includes:

1. working towards grandparents' preferred goals for themselves, their grandchildren, and their communities;

2. cultivating a strong sense of commitment and dedication to achieving these goals;

3. learning how to change grandparents' participation in their families and communities in order to accomplish these goals and to make their relationships more flexible and life-enhancing;

4. having a heartfelt concern for improving conditions for growth and fulfillment in families and communities and making efforts to realize this ideal through day-by-day action;

5. realizing that there are infinite possibilities for interpreting the special mission, which is essentially grandparents making their most unique contributions in their families and in society;

6. understanding significant ways in which we are different and alike in our values and behavior;

7. respecting the importance of emotional learning as well as intellectual education, so that efforts to fulfill the special mission will be persistent as well as consistent;

8. being willing to let people alone, or allowing them to act according to their own wishes, because the special mission is truly a grandparent responsibility rather than a mechanism to coerce others to behave in certain ways.

This list shows that the special mission of grandparents is the motor that helps grandparents to bring their individual dreams into being. Special mission grandparenting simultaneously faces inwards towards families—towards grandchildren, adult children, and other relatives—and outwards towards communities—towards religious organizations, educational institutions, and the economy. In order to be whole persons, as well as the strongest possible examples for their grandchildren, grandparents must find meaningful ways to interact with both their families and their communities, so that they can draw their grandchildren into both of these worlds. Grandparents' activities and contributions that move in these directions balance and strengthen their families and help to improve their communities.

CONTRIBUTIONS MADE

Both long and short histories of the uniqueness of grandparenting in Western and Eastern civilizations show that grandparents in all social classes, races, and ethnic groups have tended to consolidate family resources, material wealth, heirlooms, and mementos in order to pass them down from their generation to the next. To the extent that these assets are desired by members of younger generations, grandparents exert power through their distributions of goods and their legacies. Although rich families have much more material wealth than poor families, and consequently grandparents in rich families wield both more family power and more community power, other kinds of resources are valued in less privileged families, where grandparents also tend to control their distribution.

However, before civilizations were based on the accumulation of assets, and continuing in both historic and some contemporary societies, grandparents were valued and exerted influence in their families and communities primarily because they passed on wisdom and valuable practical knowledge to members of younger generations. Through the ages grandparents have been sources of family histories, family myths, folklore, and survival skills that have been learned over at least their own lifetimes. Therefore, in Western civilization, more especially in the past than in the present, grandparents were respected for their know-how and lifetime experiences, and although it is difficult to measure all the results of these kinds of exchanges between grandparents and their families, or grandparents and their communities, members of younger generations seem to have benefitted a great deal from learning from their grandparents.

Historically, many grandparents have exercised considerable power in their communities. Even though some grandparents —especially grandmothers—have not been influential outside their families, they frequently made significant contributions to community welfare as well as to family well-being.

Historical and global perspectives help us to think through some of the worthwhile possibilities for grandparents today. Because the most ancient and most widespread tradition of grandparenting is the transmission of knowledge to members of younger generations, it is appropriate to try to find meaningful ways to achieve this in contemporary families and societies. However, before we can translate this timeless tradition into modern practices, we should ask ourselves some questions that are influenced by more contemporary knowledge about human behavior:

1. What is it that grandparents know that is most helpful to their grandchildren's development and social progress?

2. What are the most effective ways for grandparents to communicate this knowledge?

3. To what extent is grandparents' know-how grounded in their own family experiences, family histories, and community relations?

4. How can grandparents have a constructive impact on their families and communities?

All in all, past contributions of grandparents are a rich source for suggestions as to what a particular special mission of a grandparent may be today, as well as grandparents' current interests. Although physical and material circumstances may change radically through time, extremes of poverty and wealth remain, as well as possibilities for establishing meaningful connections between generations. Furthermore, some elders continue to carve out significant niches for themselves in ongoing community exchanges, which become an inspiration to other grandparents. Hearing, seeing, and telling—strategies that will be discussed in detail in the next three chapters—also heighten grandparents' awareness about their opportunities to make lasting family and community contributions.

When Victor, Ella, Henry, and Sheila reflected on their families' experiences of the past, they were able to define more clearly what they wanted to do themselves. Victor looked at how his grandfather had managed to stay in touch with his family in spite of his extensive travel as a salesman; Ella reflected on her aunt's contributions to her local church; Henry remembered how his elderly relatives had helped him to value education; and Sheila traced the volunteer work of independent women in past generations of her family. This scope of interest and focused review were inspired by the idea of a special mission, which also enabled Victor, Ella, Henry, and Sheila to decide what they want to accomplish in their families and in society.

PURPOSE, MEANING, DIRECTION

Once new ideas about possibilities for a special mission as a grandparent settled into the minds and being of Victor, Ella, Henry, and Sheila, they were each able to increase and cultivate purpose, meaning, and direction in their daily behavior. Reflections about their families became emotional learning, and later emotional sustenance for their grandchildren, especially when good intentions were put into action. Thus having a special mission means adding purpose and direction to everyday decision making. This impetus allowed Victor, Ella, Henry, and Sheila to transcend banal aspects of their situations and to do what they most wanted to do.

When Victor reviewed his options for grandparenting, he realized that he first had to overcome his adult children's resistance to him, so that he could get sufficient access to his grandchildren. His sense of purpose, meaning, and direction was a dependable source of inspiration and motivation, which carried him forward in his difficult venture. He also became relatively immune to the recurring disappointments, setbacks, and criticisms which beset him while he tried to get to know his grandchildren.

Ella made several local contacts in order to discover how she could best contribute to a particular community need. Because her aunt had been active in her church congregation, Ella decided to follow in her footsteps. Ella's local church appreciated and respected her efforts to get involved, and Ella was invited to organize and supervise expanded child care services for participants in their weekly church services.

Henry was fascinated with his family's history. His special mission motivated him to ask for information from his relatives, so that he could increase his scant knowledge of family facts and past relationships. Furthermore, when Henry made contact with relatives whom he had never met before, he began to open up relationships throughout his family. A more direct consequence of Henry's project is that his grandchildren began to learn about their family's past long before Henry had a finished family history in hand.

Sheila's reflections on her women relatives' volunteer achievements inspired her to start work at a nonprofit organization that advocates women's health. Therefore, Sheila's special mission includes both cultivating strong relationships with family members and expressing her concern for women's well-being through volunteer work. Her knowledge about women's issues helps to free her grandchildren from limiting family and community stereotypes and brings them into a more expansive future.

Purpose, meaning, and direction help grandparents to break through their passivity and automatic acceptance of the limiting conventional expectations for grandparents. Specifically, purpose, meaning, and direction help grandparents to formulate

goals that they want to achieve and provide motivation to actually accomplish these goals. However, the mission must have a
large sense of purpose, meaning, and direction if it is to create
constructive consequences for grandchildren, families, and
communities. That is, it should also reach out to those who are
beyond their immediate kin networks.

The special mission of grandparents is a solid launching pad
or foundation from which to make effective grandparenting
and community contributions. Changing beliefs about constructive possibilities for grandparenting creates new values and
promotes openness and flexibility in family and community relationships. At the same time, the special mission serves as an
anchor or home base for grandparents' everyday behavior and
community contributions.

Because Victor, Ella, Henry, and Sheila embraced a special
mission as grandparents, they were able to replace their passive,
conventional conformity to grandparenting expectations with
more purposeful action. By doing so they became pioneers of
sorts in their families and communities, and their grandchildren, relatives, and members of their communities benefitted
from their examples.

Victor eventually won the trust of his children and grandchildren and became an important person in his grandchildren's
lives. Ella's church activities opened up new vistas for her grandchildren. Henry's family history became a talking point and a
living, changing document for all members of his family. It was a
tool for emotional learning among young and old relatives
alike. Finally, Sheila's know-how about gender stereotypes inspired family and community practices that opened up new possibilities for men as well as women, and for boys as well as girls.
Through all of these grandparenting and community efforts
Victor, Ella, Henry, and Sheila became distinctly more effective
grandparents than they had been before.

The special mission of grandparents is thus essentially a call to action as well as a direction to take. Any particular goal may run counter to everyday customs and may involve actively resisting restrictive stereotypes, such as the commercialized belief that grandparents are here primarily to celebrate grandchildren's birthdays by buying gifts. The special mission encourages grandparents to act in their own right, and according to their own interests, that is, to become real players in their families and communities.

3

Hearing

Although hearing an inner voice is conventionally considered to be the essence of what it means to have a vocation, relationship sources of inspiration and information are just as important as internal insights or intuition in understanding what a calling to grandparent means to you. Becoming aware that both your inner self and your social environment provide useful leads for action is a significant stage in developing the special mission of grandparents, because your responses to your internal and external worlds guide you to and through the vocation of grandparenting. Hearing your call to action in the context of the special needs and opportunities of your particular grandparenting situation is crucial.

The common denominator that underlies receiving both internal and external messages about grandparenting is the singular act of hearing. We hear a mass of complex information about the past, present, and future, and what we absorb and remember depends on whether we are listening more or less attentively. Giving our attention to particular issues, or to selected intuitive and relationship cues, influences what we choose to do and increases our motivation to accomplish preferred goals. Do we want to use what we hear to strengthen ourselves and others? Or do we want to merely get by with business as usual?

Hearing is a useful tool through which grandparents can formulate or imagine those special missions that make the most sense to them. Grandparents gain practical knowledge about behavior in their families and communities by recalling past experiences and family or community stories heard through the years. Furthermore, grandparents make more connections between their actions and family and social issues, and their actions and family and social expectations, by cultivating a habit of keeping their ears to the ground. None of us thinks or acts in a vacuum, and being aware of how our families and communities influence our attitudes and behavior enables us to neutralize their impact.

As grandparents develop a stronger sense of what is going on in their families and society through recalling past events and open-minded listening, they begin to understand more about who they are in a social context. Listening to the substance and emotional tone of family and community exchanges helps grandparents to center their lives and enables them to be more effective in their families and society.

Hearing is a way to discover family and social truths, as well as a way to assess what conditions will most benefit the growth and development of all family members. At a certain point, however, hearing through recall or impromptu eavesdropping is not enough. Grandparents need to refresh and renew the family stories they know by checking them out with other relatives. Hearing what family members you have never met have to say is a particularly effective way to separate family facts from myths, because the perspectives of those who are outside the domains of habitual exchanges in families are refreshingly different and frequently ring true. Debunking family beliefs frees individuals from their relatives' pressures to conform with family beliefs and from their overinvolvement in what these individuals do.

Alphonso, Diedra, Tom, and Jackie knew very little about their grandparents when they were young. All four of Alphonso's grandparents had died before he was born; Diedra knew only one set of grandparents; Tom's grandparents died when he was a small child; and Jackie knew only her mother's mother, until this grandmother died when Jackie was a teenager. Both special mission grandparents and special agent grandparents describe grandparenting behavior which focuses on making changes in their families and these terms can be used synonymously. Therefore, Alphonso's, Diedra's, Tom's, and Jackie's knowledge about their grandparents is largely hearsay. That is, they know their grandparents through listening to what relatives say about them, rather than through their own personal relationships or direct experiences with them.

"I didn't have much of a family when I was a boy—only my parents, brothers, and sisters," Alphonso says wistfully. "Never having had grandparents makes me uninterested in grandparenting."

Diedra laments, "I knew my father's parents but not my mother's parents, but I always missed my dead grandparents, even though the grandparents I had loved me a lot. I guess I'm immature or needy for attention."

"Don't talk to me about grandparents and being a grandparent," exclaims Tom. "I don't see why people get so excited about their grandchildren. I didn't have much to do with my grandparents, and I grew up just fine."

Jackie says longingly, "I think having only Nanna made me want to be a wonderful grandmother just like her. I didn't feel deprived by having only one grandparent—it just made me want to be a grandmother myself someday."

Given their lack of grandparenting experiences when they were young, Alphonso and Tom perhaps would not have seriously considered becoming special mission or special agent grandparents unless they were involved in their own family crises. Alphonso's son had been injured in a car accident within the last year, and Alphonso desperately needed financial support and hands-on assistance with child care in order to raise his two young sons. Tom's family crisis was that his seventeen-year-old daughter had recently given birth to a baby girl, after her unstable relationship with another teenager ended. Tom's daughter wants her parents to let her live at home with her baby until she finishes high school and gets a job. Although Tom's wife supports her daughter's wish to do this, Tom refuses to help her. He feels disappointed, exploited, and emotionally removed from his role as a grandfather.

Listening to what other relatives said about these family crises, or listening to advice about how to make things better, helped both Alphonso and Tom to understand that difficult circumstances often bring families closer together. Alphonso and Tom also heard how many grandparents help their children in one way or another, even though their assistance is often unheralded because it is neither visible nor particularly newsworthy.

Hearing was also a useful tool for Diedra and Jackie to become special agent grandparents, although Diedra gradually recognized that grandparenting had limits through hearing more about her other grandparents. She also began to realize more fully how much the only grandparents she had known had tried to be there for her. For her part, Jackie gained a fuller appreciation of what grandparenting means by listening to family stories about her three long-deceased grandparents and by paying more attention to what she hears about grandparents in her neighborhood.

If you want to strengthen your influence as a grandparent, you and your grandchildren will benefit from your being as objective as possible about your current circumstances, as well as benefitting from your remaining actively committed to your own values and interests. Keeping your ears open helps you to understand the kinds of contributions grandparents make in their families and communities and, at the same time, enables you to break through any personal idiosyncrasies and biases that limit your expectations and aspirations. When you hear your family and community relationship facts more clearly, you will be able to be more realistic about who you are and about what your expectations and aspirations are or could be. Furthermore, you will be able to question the assumptions you make about purpose, meaning, and direction in your daily activities, as well as become the kind of grandparent you really want to be.

Thus the tool of hearing draws us out of ourselves and gives us more choices in our behavior than merely reacting to what others demand or expect of us, however needy they may be. Our horizons broaden when we deliberately recall the past and try to connect our knowledge of the past with what is going on in the present. Hearing what our relatives say helps us to manage our energy and commitments to our families and communities more effectively.

Listening to information about their families' pasts and their grandparents' contributions in different social settings helped Alphonso, Diedra, Tom, and Jackie to develop their own grandparenting styles more freely. Putting their current relationships into the context of the intricate webs of intergenerational exchanges in their families and communities helps them to understand more fully why they are not victims because they did not have long-standing relationships with their grandparents when they were children. Becoming more aware of these broad relationship connections also increased their emotional security and, essentially, reassured them that they can be effective grandparents now, whatever their past grandparenting experiences were.

Asking questions and listening to relatives' and community members' answers filled in gaps in their knowledge about their families and communities, as well as provided valuable emotional resources for dealing with present stresses. When he became more involved with his family, Alphonso increased his interest in grandparenting, and he became sufficiently motivated to carry through with a special mission to help his son and his family. Hearing what his relatives and neighbors had to say about his daughter's situation allowed Tom to slowly come to terms with the facts that many children have been raised successfully by single parents and that his daughter and grandchild would survive this critical period more successfully with his support than without it.

Hearing information about her family and her community also allowed Diedra to be more knowledgeable about ways to meet her own emotional needs as well as those of her grandchildren. Lastly, when Jackie heard how other grandparents relate to their grandchildren, her experiences with her grandmother no longer limited her grandparenting attitudes and behavior as much as before.

HEARING FROM THE PAST

In order to come through with positive results Alphonso, Diedra, Tom, and Jackie had to use different ways to hear and understand which of their past patterns of family and community behavior influenced and restricted their current situations most. Alphonso made contact with other family elders so that he could be more informed about past events and relationships in his family. Hearing more about these past generations led Alphonso to make contact with relatives he never even knew existed. Diedra started to talk to relatives and friends of the grandparents she had known, and she also made new friends for herself in her local neighborhood. These friends supported Diedra in her quest to lead a more satisfying life as a grandmother. Tom reestablished contact with his cousins in order to find out more about the grandparents he had lost when he was a child. Pooling memories with his cousins gave Tom a fuller picture of the grandparents they shared and deepened his understanding of his family's dynamics. Meanwhile Jackie explored who her other grandparents had been and what they had done. Listening to countless family stories about these grandparents strengthened her sense of them and herself as real people.

Opening up new channels of hearing and understanding the past broadened the emotional bases or family foundations of Alphonso, Diedra, Tom, and Jackie. Hearing relatives' memories and family stories of the past also reawakened and extended their short-lived experiences of their grandparents. Thus strengthening connections with the past clarifies present relationships and pressures. Hearing from the past allowed Alphonso, Diedra, Tom, and Jackie to become more meaningfully oriented to the future, especially with regard to their roles and responsibilities as grandparents.

The following principles sum up special mission grandparents' benefits from hearing about the past:

1. knowledge of a family's past can inspire individuals to become special mission grandparents;
2. oral histories, stories about families, or conversations about deceased relatives are emotional resources that can increase motivation to become a special mission grandparent;
3. hearing different relatives' perspectives on past family and community dynamics can strengthen ongoing family and community relationships;
4. hearing from the past creates a strategic and valuable know-how that can be passed on to grandchildren;
5. techniques that enhance hearing from the past increase abilities to keep up with and manage responses to current family issues.

Alphonso, Diedra, Tom, and Jackie strengthened their interest and enthusiasm for being grandparents by making deliberate efforts to hear from the past. Their improved hearing of past facts about their families and communities heightened their ca-

pacities to hear useful clues for future fulfillment and contributions. Consequently they became not only skilled listeners, but
also thoughtful and effective actors in their families and communities.

HEARING FOR THE FUTURE

In order to be wise visionaries for the future, the best preparation for grandparents is to cultivate an appreciation of life's
big issues through hearing from the past. Special mission grandparents realize, sooner or later, that understanding past family
dynamics enables them to deal maturely with present issues and
dilemmas in their family relationships. Furthermore, creating a
consciously lived historical perspective, through listening to
community members' comments about the past as well as those
of relatives, enhances and strengthens their future contributions to their communities.

Hearing for the future includes being alert to new opportunities as well as understanding the limitations of past and current circumstances. Alphonso knows that mourning for the
losses of his childhood will not carry him forward in the long
run and that in order for him to bring the best of all his possible
worlds into being, he has to make the most of his current family relationships and community resources. Diedra came to
recognize that she has a responsibility to meet her own present
and future needs and that grieving for the past is unproductive
for both her and her grandchildren. Tom realized that he
would be stronger if he embraced his crisis grandparenting
possibilities now, rather than rejecting or denying them, and
that he could help his daughter and his granddaughter more if
he was truly positive about this commitment. Defining his special mission clearly along these lines motivated Tom sufficiently to be able to persist in his efforts to respond to his
daughter's predicament positively. Jackie also found that letting go of her restricted experiences of the past opened up

family and community opportunities for the future. When she was less rigid about conforming to what she thought she should do, Jackie became a more effective grandmother and made more meaningful community contributions through her work as a nurse.

Although no one can be a reliable visionary of the future, special mission grandparents develop their hunches about constructive possibilities for the future through hearing what is going on now and by connecting their ongoing listening with what they have heard about the past. In these respects, special mission grandparents

1. nurture that which is emotionally significant to them and their grandchildren;
2. maintain a constructive orientation to ongoing family and community conditions, whatever they are;
3. help their grandchildren to develop a positive and creative posture to life;
4. confront relatives and members of their communities with practical suggestions when what they have heard and understood requires challenging the status quo;
5. teach others how to survive present pressures, as well as how to find meaning and fulfillment in the future;
6. ask others for help and pay attention to what they hear;
7. respond appropriately to those who ask them for guidance;
8. cultivate meaning, purpose, and direction to carry them forward into an improved future;
9. hear truth rather than lies, and organize their lives around honest, thoughtful priorities;
10. support grandchildren and others in their efforts to achieve their dreams.

Life is an ongoing process, and special mission grandparents are in the best position possible to realize intergenerational continuities in families and communities and to act on values that improve the human condition. Our futures are built through the myriad decisions we make in the present, and being a special mission grandparent increases the likelihood that we will act effectively for ourselves, our families, and our communities.

Alphonso, Diedra, Tom, and Jackie were able to build sufficiently strong bases of family and community knowledge to be able to move into their respective futures with confidence. Honing their hearing skills helped them to understand how their family and community dependencies influenced their behavior, and this know-how slowly and surely protected them from being exploited, isolated, or ignored. They became stronger actors in their own right when they paid attention to past and present complexities in their families and communities, and they heard more clearly what they needed to do in order to have more satisfying futures.

Alphonso not only responded to his son's needs, but he also changed his job and moved into a position that allowed him to do more meaningful work. He became stronger as a person, and he had a more positive impact in his community as well as in his family. Tom decided to support his daughter, and in addition, he volunteered to mentor troubled teenagers in his community. By becoming more concerned about others, and being actively involved in increasing their well-being, Tom was happier and gained respect.

For her part, Diedra decided to become her family's historian, and in addition, she made many new friendships outside her family. Making an increased number of meaningful contacts gave Diedra stronger emotional roots, greater security, and more opportunities to express her concerns and make contributions to others. Jackie was increasingly successful in her profession as a nurse, and she helped her grandchildren to make equally significant career decisions for themselves. Jackie's zest for her special mission as a grandparent also helped her grand-children to be more enthusiastic about their opportunities and responsibilities to better themselves, their families, and their communities.

Although merely listening carefully to varied sources in dif-ferent times and contrasting situations helps to bring about many constructive results, it is also important to know that see-ing and telling are two additional tools that facilitate and expe-dite the efforts of grandparents. Thus hearing, seeing, and telling are complementary starting points that together deepen individuals' positive responses to the special mission of grand-parents.

Because no single perspective or approach guarantees constructive long-term results in grandparenting, hearing must be considered as a tool that may or may not be used together with seeing or telling strategies. The main advantage of using these tools as starting points in planning and undertaking special missions as grandparents is that the techniques of hearing, seeing, and telling yield increased possibilities and options. The next two chapters suggest how grandparents may apply these three perspectives singly or together in everyday situations.

4

Seeing

The special mission of grandparents takes on a life of its own when these grandparents begin to see themselves and their relationships differently. Furthermore, these grandparents are more able to see opportunities for modifying their behavior in their families and in their communities than are other grandparents, because of their stronger orientation and motivation to make constructive changes. Although this kind of seeing necessarily involves seeing with an inner eye through understanding and intuition, as well as physiological three-dimensional sight, all kinds of seeing can be thought of as a tool—in addition to the tools of hearing and telling—that enables grandparents to become more effective and to have a greater impact on others.

As in the case of the tool of hearing, grandparents are able to use the tool of seeing more deliberately when they increase their alertness to what they see in their social environments—particularly in their families and communities—as well as to what they see through reflecting about observations they have already made. The particular usefulness of the tool of seeing is that it allows grandparents to find and make connections between their different worlds, so that they can choose family and community strategies more skillfully, and consequently act more meaningfully.

Also as with the tool of hearing, seeing may be accomplished vicariously as well as individually. We often increase our visual understanding of complex situations by knowing what others see and communicate, as well as through our own observations, whether the actual sharing of vision and insights takes place through writing letters or journals; drawing pictures or plans; taking photographs; collecting heirlooms; perusing legal documents such as wills or contracts; examining records of births, marriages, and deaths; looking at mementos; or exchanging E-mail. Although many family and community members do not have access to computers, they can still find a wide variety of ways and means to make meaningful visual or symbolic communications with each other about themselves, their relationships, and their living conditions.

In everyday conversation we frequently refer to seeing the broader picture of our particular problems or situations. Seeing the intricacies of our family and community networks is a significant and necessary phase of formulating effective contributions to our families and communities. Interestingly enough, this kind of panoramic seeing is often easier for grandparents to accomplish, given their particular intergenerational location in complex relationships systems, than for others. Also, because grandparents are linked more directly and more closely to their past generations, family lineages, and community histories than other family members, grandparents' views are larger and more rooted in the past.

Ishmael, Sara, Yunho, and Ellen are doting grandparents who want to do what is best for their grandchildren. Ishmael and Sara, who have been married to each other for more than thirty years, cling to family traditions to guide them in grandparenting their four grandsons. They believe that a strict religious upbringing will give their grandsons a firm foundation that will show them the way through life whatever their circumstances may be. They teach their grandsons as much as possible about conservative Judaism through using books, the Hebrew language, and religious symbols.

Yunho is also a great believer in tradition. During much of the time Yunho spends with his grandchildren, he helps them to imagine what it is like to live in China and what Chinese families are like. Yunho's parents immigrated to the United States when they were young, and they kept their memories of China alive through showing their children many family mementos and souvenirs from China.

By contrast, Ellen wants her grandchildren to move with modern times through understanding and acting in response to contemporary conditions. She became perhaps too independent from her family herself as a young adult, and her vision of her grandchildren's future possibilities revolves around her past and ongoing struggles to survive as a professional woman with a small business.

> "The thing that matters most in life is religion," says Ishmael. "When I teach Judaism to my grandsons, I am very happy."
>
> "I want my grandsons to have Jewish homes when they grow up," says Sara. "A child is never too young to pray or take part in Jewish rituals."
>
> Yunho reminisces, "My parents gave me a very lively picture of what China is like, and this is what I want to do for my grandchildren. Also, if they know a lot about real Chinese families, they will be able to have their own Chinese families."
>
> Ellen is more questioning in her approach to grandparenting. "I don't know what kind of families work best," she says. "All I know is that I want my grandchildren to enjoy life. I hope they will treat people well, look after themselves, and help to make the world a better place."

Ishmael, Sara, Yunho, and Ellen each have a vision of what they want to do for and with their grandchildren. Ishmael and Sara have many points of overlap and agreement in their visions.

Like Ishmael and Sara, Yunho has a traditional view of what he wants to give his grandchildren. For her part, however, Ellen is more open-minded towards change than Ishmael, Sara, and Yunho, especially when she sees what possibilities and opportunities are available for her grandchildren today. Although Ellen has a more ambiguous vision of her role as a grandparent than Ishmael, Sara, or Yunho, she sees herself clearly as a pioneer or an explorer. Ellen wants herself and her grandchildren to find ways to better the human condition rather than uphold tradition.

Special mission grandparents strengthen their capacities to see reality and work towards bringing a more constructive future into being. They not only become increasingly aware of past relationships in their families and communities, including family and community traditions, but they also keep up with contemporary changes by playing significant roles in future-directed family and community actions. The special mission of grandparents is thus a call to action that is inclusive rather than exclusive. That is, these grandparents strive towards achieving the well-being of total families, whole communities, or whole societies, rather than the survival or excellence of one particular group. Their actions are based on the broadest possible visions of realities and opportunities.

Seeing is a tool that can transport us to both the past and the future. Seeing in the present is a way to begin to understand the past and to start to plan for the future. Although Ishmael, Sara, and Yunho are already adept at seeing the past, it is difficult for them to apply their visions to the present and future in meaningful ways. Ellen's view of the past may be unduly distorted by her painful professional struggles, but she understands more clearly than Ishmael, Sara, and Yunho that the past is largely a source of inspiration for making appropriate and constructive changes to shared traditions in the present and for the future. Ellen's vision is also based more on her knowledge of society as a whole than that of Ishmael, Sara, or Yunho, so her special mission actions are more likely to have a lasting impact on others.

Seeing is therefore a tool that special mission grandparents use to accomplish at least some of the following:

1. seeing provides a vision that can give grandparents purpose, meaning, and direction in their daily lives;

2. seeing deepens understanding of families and communities, so that the actions of grandparents become more effective;

3. seeing is a meaningful mode of communication—among relatives or among community members—that distills much information and consequently enlarges the perspectives of all concerned;

4. seeing is a vital personal experience that helps to both reconstruct the past and imagine the future;

5. seeing is a means of change, because shedding new light on established family and community problems suggests ways to solve them;

6. seeing is one of our earliest symbolic communications with others, a primal kind of recognition that goes deeper than verbal exchanges and transcends conversation.

SEEING FROM THE PAST

We see from the past most accurately and most effectively when we see not only with our own eyes, but also through the eyes and experiences of others. Building a family archive and collecting community records provide invaluable collective views of the past and present. Also, informally ordering photographs of relatives, or photocopying old letters that were sent between family members, creates a unique picture of a family's past and present.

Because grandparents are usually more familiar with the names and personal particulars of their deceased relatives and their closest relationships, they are more able to put a meaningful picture together from assorted family heirlooms or mementos. This is important because the symbolism of family exchanges in the past can yield vital meanings for today's relationships and conflicts. For example, we begin to understand why certain parts of a family have been estranged from the rest when we read family wills or when we scrutinize photographs of family reunions. In part, grandparents may be more astute at interpreting visual materials than other family members because they frequently have more time, more patience, and more interest in deciphering both obvious and hidden meanings about their families and communities.

Ishmael, Sara, and Yunho are tightly tied to the past. They are familiar with many repeated patterns of behavior through the generations of their families, and each has vivid personal memories of grandparents, great-aunts, or great-uncles. However, they tend to be preoccupied with their connections to the past, and they spend inordinate amounts of energy amassing family mementos and other kinds of inherited religious or cultural symbols that have been passed down by deceased relatives. This strong focus on the past restricts their openness to the present and the future.

On the other hand, Ellen has kept relatively few souvenirs of her family's history. Because pictures and objects that belonged to her grandparents did not evoke pleasant childhood memories for her, she has spent much of her adult life trying to put these kinds of reminders of the past behind her. Furthermore, when Ellen reflects about the course of her life, she does not make any connection between what was essentially her rejection of her closest family relationships and her intense struggles as a professional woman. It can be surmised, however, that Ellen's comparative lack of emotional moorings in her family made her particularly susceptible and vulnerable to becoming a victim of tensions in the workplace.

Special mission grandparents try to see the past for what it is—an unchangeable legacy—and bring it to bear on present-day decisions and actions as constructively as possible. Understanding the complexity of relationships among previous generations ultimately frees them to be who they want to be and to accomplish their own goals.

Through time Ishmael, Sara, and Yunho were able to loosen their riveted and rather rigid visions of the past by seeing that the tenacity of their bonds to past family dependencies restricted their abilities to be autonomous in the present. When they realized that seeing from the past is only one part of being responsible grandparents in the present, they became less provincial and less demanding in their relationships with their grandchildren.

For her part, Ellen began to understand that seeing the past could increase her effectiveness as a grandparent and as a businesswoman. By paying more attention to her family's past, she not only sees how trapped women in prior generations of her family have been, but also how some of them managed to increase their independence in spite of these limitations. Ellen also sees that a history of her local community reveals many insular attitudes and mediocre accomplishments. As a result of examining these past facts, Ellen was able to reevaluate her present possibilities. Taking this broader view encouraged her to pursue her chosen goals with greater courage and more persistence than she had been able to before.

SEEING FOR THE FUTURE

Vision is an effective tool for accomplishing family and community changes. Whether we see ourselves as traditional or conventional grandparents, or as special mission grandparents, our views of ourselves have a strong influence on what we do. Who we think we are and who we want to be both depend on how we see ourselves. The decisions we make and the actions we take flow from how we see ourselves and our options, and being true to how we see ourselves brings greater freedom and increased effectiveness in our present and future behavior. We also make more long-standing contributions to our families and our communities when we deliberately formulate our own visions of ourselves and our goals.

The influence our visions have on our behavior suggests that when we are sufficiently aware, we see ways to be and ways to accomplish our future goals. Thus heightening our awareness as special mission grandparents gradually propels us into actions that will ultimately better our families and our communities.

When Ishmael tried to live out his special mission as a grandfather, he became more adept at seeing how his strong religious beliefs could be reconnected to broad social issues. He not only continued to teach his grandsons about Judaism, but also volunteered to teach in the religious school at his synagogue. Meeting more Jewish families gave him an impetus to extend his audience even further, to include his giving speeches at local community gatherings and addresses at neighboring public schools. As Ishmael broadened his interests and contributions he became more responsive to his grandsons' emotional needs, and he participated in more varied activities with them.

Sara also followed some of her own interests in a wider community. She became active in a foster grandparent program and urged her grandsons to get involved in this work. As Sara moved into a bigger world, her grandsons benefitted from her desire to have a better future through seeing and addressing the needs of those outside their family. Sara's grandsons could see a world and life that went beyond—but was still connected to—their Jewish family.

Becoming a special mission grandparent also helped Yunho to look at the future more responsibly. Yunho began to realize that the tenacity of his hold on Chinese traditions was largely a denial of recent political and cultural changes in China and that re-creating his grandparents' and parents' visions of China may not be very useful to his grandchildren today. Although Yunho did not want to assimilate into the culture of the United States, he began to make friends within local Chinese communities. As a result of these extended contacts Yunho saw more possibilities to cooperate with American friends as well as Chinese friends. By introducing his grandchildren to his new world, he enabled them to both cherish their Chinese origins and value the opportunities that are available to them now. Thus Yunho's grandchildren found new ways to be different, as well as to continue to respect and share their Chinese traditions and heritage.

Ellen's way to see for the future included describing her deceased women relatives to her grandchildren and using her women relatives' independent behavior as a base from which she could make new kinds of contributions. Ellen found that these personal examples of richly lived experiences in her family inspire her grandsons and granddaughters and awaken their own connectedness to the past. Ellen was gradually able to focus more effectively on her own professional goals, and she used a vision of possibilities that encompassed her relatives' experiences to guide her actions. Her expanded family base increased her emotional security, so that she was able to move forward and make more of an impact than she had been able to before becoming a special mission grandparent.

In summary, special mission grandparents use seeing to help them to lead more meaningful lives. Even though grandparenting can be enjoyable in its own right, whatever the mode of grandparenting, there are always many advantages to seeing additional grandparenting options and possibilities. Becoming aware of some of the many opportunities for special mission grandparents includes:

1. seeing connections between past, present, and future patterns of behavior in your families;

2. seeing connections between past, present, and future patterns of meaningful behavior in your communities;

3. seeing connections between your family, local neighborhood, nearest city, and your country at this present point in history and using this knowledge to work out what kinds of contributions you want to make;

4. seeing how to use your expanding knowledge of the universe to communicate with your grandchildren.

Ishmael, Sara, Yunho, and Ellen were able to broaden their worlds and change their visions of grandparenting through defining special missions for themselves. This process made them more true to their real selves rather than less authentic, and their grandchildren, families, and communities benefitted from their different contributions.

Ishmael was able to balance his life more effectively with regard to his deep religious beliefs and community responsibilities. His view of the world included more concern for secular conditions in society, and his recognized teaching skills became an entree for getting more deeply involved in his local community.

Sara's work with a local foster grandparent program helped her to break out of the safe cocoon of her family. As she tried to meet others' family needs, her world opened up, and her grandsons were able to see how important it is to understand and alleviate the predicaments of those who are less advantaged than they are. They were also more able to see how Sara's religious faith gave her courage and stamina to cross these social boundaries.

Yunho's contacts with Chinese communities ultimately yielded business contacts as well as new friends, and he became more happily assimilated into American society without losing his Chinese identity. He learned much more about conditions in contemporary China from lectures, informal contacts, and conversations within the Chinese communities, and he was able to pass on this rich knowledge to his grandchildren. The additional exchanges in his Chinese world also made Yunho more flexible and more open-minded in his dealings with his grandchildren.

Ellen's newfound appreciation of her family roots motivated her to take a more in-depth, patient attitude to her professional conflicts. Her deeper and more extended base of emotional security increased her resistance to annoyance, and she was able to be more philosophical about her goals and expectations. Her grandchildren welcomed Ellen's new laid-back approach to herself and them, and they enjoyed spending time with her more than they had before. They learned much from her example of patience and fortitude, and they became more interested in their family history themselves.

In order to more fully integrate hearing, seeing, and telling techniques that help individuals to become special mission grandparents, the following chapter is devoted to examining the advantages of telling. Telling is a way to develop new knowledge, revive and create meaningful family bonds, and build loyalties. Although hearing and seeing are necessarily closely related, and cannot be separated from telling, it is practical to think of each approach to understanding and forming family or community relationships as a significant starting point for becoming a special mission grandparent.

5

Telling

Telling is the third strategic starting point for becoming a special mission grandparent. Together with hearing and seeing, telling is a tool that heightens grandparents' awareness, deepens their understanding, and increases their knowledge about past and current relationships.

Special mission grandparents play significant roles in their families and communities. Because grandparents have a unique intergenerational position, they frequently know a great deal about key players in their families and communities, as well as about significant past issues. However, it is not enough for grandparents to cling to their family and community wisdom or to use it only when called upon to do so. They increase the effectiveness of their contributions by making their knowledge of family stories, family histories, and past community events available to others. Special mission grandparents accumulate relevant information continuously, influence current family and community concerns by initiating varied interpersonal contacts, and actively tell others what they know and what they believe.

Not all family members or members of communities want to either hear or consider the knowledge that special mission grandparents have. Therefore, grandparents' particular challenge is to find creative and innovative ways to describe important historical facts, so that the information they have will be heard and absorbed rather than rejected. Through devising specific means—like recording family histories on tape, or distributing family newsletters—and through making appropriate repetitions, especially when faced with resistant listeners, grandparents make progress in telling it how it was or how it is.

The key to telling meaningful facts effectively is to choose the right time and the right situation to describe what went on in the past. Ideally, most telling should take place in an emotional ambience that is more or less receptive to what is being told, however skillfully a grandparent may have put the facts together. However, if telling is done in a more or less frozen form—like videotapes or audiotapes—choosing the moment to tell may no longer be in the hands of the raconteur.

One of the requirements of effective telling is that it be light-hearted in tone, so that it is not reduced merely to a way to tell others what to do. Humor, imaginative asides about familiar relationships, and irreverent comparisons increase the liveliness of the family stories grandparents tell and increase the capacity of their listeners to hear what they are really saying. As long as the truth is not too outrageously embellished, or too distorted, some significant meaning will be transmitted—and, it is hoped, heard—through these kinds of informal, nonthreatening narratives.

Mercedes, Henrique, Laura, and Keith have a fair amount of information about their families, but they are reluctant to talk about the past with their grandchildren. They want their grandchildren to think of them as modern grandparents, so they almost exclusively discuss current concerns with them. Mercedes, Henrique, Laura, and Keith deal with the past in this way partly because they feel insecure about their worth in their families and communities and, partly, because they do not think that what they have to say is important.

Mercedes and Henrique have been married to each other for twenty-eight years. They lived in Venezuela before they immigrated to the United States, and through the course of time they have blotted out many memories of Venezuela. Because of the mistiness of their past, they do not tell their grandchildren much about the old country. However, in spite of their own apprehensions, their American grandchildren think that they are very interesting people.

Laura is ashamed of having been divorced twice. When her grandchildren were young, she hid this information from them, but now that they are old enough to ask questions, she feels obliged to give them at least some bare-bones facts about her failed marriages. Although undoubtedly Laura's grandchildren benefit from knowing what her experiences in these relationships were, Laura does not think she sets a good example for them, and she does not divulge any details about her divorces.

Keith has never had much to do with his family. It is only because his daughter wants her children to have a grandfather that he has reluctantly agreed to try to relate to them. However, Keith does not take much initiative to see or take out his grandchildren, and consequently they do not pay him much attention. Keith is fairly satisfied with his passive style of grandparenting, but his daughter is angry at what she considers to be his lack of interest in his grandchildren. Keith's concerns about his conflict with his daughter have increased because he does not know how to break though his apathy. He feels unable to build meaningful bonds with his grandchildren and daughter, even though he would like to do so.

Mercedes, Henrique, Laura, and Keith had interesting but not very inspiring responses to a suggestion that their roles as grandparents would be more meaningful if they would try to tell their grandchildren more about their own backgrounds. They resisted this strategy because it was difficult for them to understand how communicating this kind of personal historical information could improve their relationships with their grandchildren on a daily basis.

"I haven't thought much about describing our lives in Venezuela to our grandchildren," says Mercedes. "Anyway, how could they really be interested in what we did there? It's been so long since we were in Venezuela, and there must have been many changes. We have completely rebuilt our lives since we came to the States, so surely it is being here that counts most."

"I can't remember much about my family in Venezuela," says Henrique wistfully. "We lost touch with many of our relatives after we came to the United States. We are the only ones from our families to emigrate, and no one has ever come here to visit us. It was too expensive for us to return to Venezuela on a regular basis, and after a while the phone calls weren't enough, especially after our parents died."

"I am quite ashamed that I couldn't make my marriages work," Laura says. "I don't want to discuss my past, and I am sure my grandchildren would not be interested to know what I did wrong, or how my marriages failed. I just want to forget everything about that part of my life, so that I can really make the most of what I have today."

"Actually, I don't even like to spend time with my family," exclaims Keith. "I try to have some kind of relationship with my grandchildren because my daughter wants me to, but I will never understand why she tries to get me involved, or why anyone gets so caught up with their families."

These are not very auspicious starting points for Mercedes, Henrique, Laura, and Keith to create meaningful special missions as grandparents. However, something positive can always be derived from the past, and discussing these kinds of difficult experiences is useful. The challenge for Mercedes, Henrique, Laura, and Keith is to discover what is most significant about the past and present, which they can then pass on to their grandchildren. Their grandchildren will inevitably benefit from getting to know what went on through the generations before them, because telling them how it was clears the way for them to be more constructive in the present and reduces the likelihood that they will get into useless repetitions of this behavior in the future. The negative chain reactions that usually occur between generations in the same family are irretrievably broken by telling initiatives that special mission grandparents take. Telling opens up family and community opportunities for grandchildren and others.

Telling can be usefully thought of as the ultimate expression of successful hearing and seeing in families and communities. Grandparents activate their memories and heighten their awareness by hearing and seeing, and they pass on their accumulated knowledge to future generations through telling. Grandchildren, relatives, and community members benefit from special mission grandparents' telling through expanding their know-how for dealing with people effectively and making constructive changes.

Telling engages people in acts of constructing and deconstructing the past and in imagining the future from the present. Telling increases motivation to be special mission grandparents, as well as broadens the scope of grandparents' family and community exchanges. The cross-fertilization of ideas that occurs through telling increases progress in a quest for objectivity and truth because hearing, seeing, and telling sharpen our perspectives on past, present, and future realities.

Looking at some of the optimal conditions and consequences of telling is necessary for assessing when and what we should tell other family members. Although Mercedes, Henrique, Laura, and Keith had different reasons as to why they do not want to tell their grandchildren more than a minimum about the past, being aware of the benefits of telling encourages grandparents to open up to these possibilities:

1. telling makes family and community relationships more meaningful;

2. telling enriches the substance of everyday exchanges, and strengthens family and community bonds;

3. telling fills in gaps in histories and knowledge, and makes wisdom and know-how more accessible to members of young generations;

4. telling expresses the fruits of hearing and seeing, so that grandparents become more purposeful in their communications;

5. telling moves grandparents in a direction of making constructive changes in family and community relationships, and all participants benefit from having more open exchanges;

6. telling consolidates information so that family and community histories go beyond simple descriptions;

7. telling is a means to achieve objectivity and truth, which reduces suffering due to distortions and stereotypes;

8. telling bridges families and communities, and introduces members of young generations to the world at large;

9. telling constructs new memories, through which innovative visions are designed and transmitted to future generations;

10. telling equalizes or levels relationships, so that the parties involved grow from clarifying their communications.

Mercedes, Henrique, Laura, and Keith expanded their universes and brought about constructive changes in their families through telling their grandchildren about themselves. Even though they had not been eager to do this, once they tried to interest their grandchildren in their past lives, they found that their relationships with them became more meaningful, more resilient, and more tenacious. Mercedes, Henrique, Laura, and Keith were able to use telling as a way to help them to understand the past and as a means to prepare them for the future.

TELLING FROM THE PAST

Because families and communities do not usually have written or agreed-upon histories, the ways in which stories about the past are told is particularly important. In fact, power in families and communities often lies in the hands of those who know the most about these histories.

Putting together an accurate portrayal of the past is ideally a collective effort. No single individual's view of what has happened is sufficient to see the whole picture. Therefore, grandparents who want to understand the past contact as many relatives or community members as possible, in order to have them share in telling about the past.

Mercedes started to telephone and write to relatives she had not spoken to for many years, so that she can collect more information about her family in Venezuela. She got to know what happened after she left her home in Venezuela and was saddened to learn how many of her close relatives had died during the last twenty years. Mercedes also began to get to know her nieces and nephews through this kind of telling, as well as their children and the spouses of her previously unmarried siblings and cousins.

Henrique followed Mercedes' example, and he also made his own contacts with long-lost relatives and new family members. Henrique became so interested in catching up with information about his family that he decided to get involved in his youngest brother's business in Venezuela. Within a few months he arranged for himself and Mercedes to visit Venezuela, which was only their second visit since they emigrated. Henrique viewed this trip as a golden opportunity for him to tell his family about what he has been doing all these years and to make plans for his grandchildren to travel to Venezuela at a later time.

Laura mustered up sufficient courage to take a long hard look at the kind of life her relatives had led in the immediate past. As she gathered information about her parent and grand-parent generations, she began to realize that she was by no means alone in having difficulty with her marriages. In fact, her experience of two conflictual marriages and two fairly amicable divorces was much more tolerable than the abusive relation-ships many women in her family had suffered. Although having a rather sordid family history did not make Laura feel good, it helped her to gain a more balanced perspective on her own problems. Also, she knew that she had become stronger and more mature because of her unfortunate experiences. Listening to her relatives tell her about their pain made Laura more confi-dent about the wisdom of passing on her relationship knowl-edge to her grandchildren. She began to understand why telling them about her past could help them to have more satisfying re-lationships than she had.

Keith began to talk to relatives beyond his daughter about his difficulties in maintaining his family ties. He found that his older brother also has many negative feelings about his family and that he too is finding it burdensome to be a grandparent. Talking to his youngest sister gave Keith more details about how his parents had related to one another in the last years of their lives, and getting this information inspired him to keep in touch with his brothers and sisters more regularly in the future. The extended base of his connectedness with his family moti-vated Keith to seek out his grandchildren more and to become more deeply involved in their lives.

Thus telling from the past helped Mercedes, Henrique, Laura, and Keith to establish firmer foundations for their family relationships. Widening their worlds brought new perspectives to the challenge of becoming special mission grandparents and increased their interest in their communities as well as in their families.

TELLING FOR THE FUTURE

One of the most constructive and most proactive things that special mission grandparents do is to tell about the past and the present to their grandchildren, in order to prepare them for the future. Because the end of their lives is in sight, grandparents frequently decide to make the most of the present by investing in the future through their grandchildren. By communicating the fruits of their hearing and seeing through telling, grandparents increase meaning, purpose, and direction in their lives and in the lives of others.

Special mission grandparents make mature value choices. They realize that a long life brings with it responsibilities to give back to their families and their communities and that telling is an energizing way to do this. Grandparents' telling for the future not only enhances the life chances of their grandchildren, but also improves their own situations.

As Mercedes, Henrique, Laura, and Keith gain a fuller appreciation of the past through their individual investigations into family and community dynamics, they understand how past behavior influences present and future conditions. This kind of distillation of the information they have gathered becomes a dynamic starting point or launching pad for their future-oriented actions.

Mercedes' views of her past inspired her to try to pass on Venezuelan customs to her grandchildren, so that they will strengthen their attachment to their family origins. Henrique's business interests provide occasions for his grandchildren to visit Venezuela, and they are developing their own contacts and experiences there. Laura introduced her children and grandchildren to some of her stepchildren, which meant that her divorces were no longer hidden. Through renewing his relationships with his brothers and sisters, Keith strengthened his family bonds. Telling his grandchildren about his family soon improved his relationships with his grandchildren.

Getting grandchildren connected to past generations of their families is a worthwhile investment in the future. When grandchildren know or know about many of their family members, they are less likely to cut themselves off from their relatives and suffer fewer negative consequences from emotional estrangements. This clearer sense of belonging to their families protects grandchildren from the strong negative influences of destructive peer groups, addictive behavior, and abusive relationships.

Mercedes encouraged her grandchildren to participate in events organized by Latin American groups in the United States. These new cultural contacts are inspirational to them and enrich their education. Henrique made arrangements for his grandchildren to visit Venezuela regularly, and they are welcomed by kin and communities that help them to transcend their American roots.

Laura's grandchildren made lasting friendships with some of her past in-laws and stepfamilies. These relationships were salvaged from Laura's past so that they could all share a more constructive future. Keith's grandchildren met relatives their own age through Keith's family contacts. Thus Keith's extended kin lines reached into the future as well as the past.

Telling is a great synthesizer for grandparents. They are supremely active when they choose to tell their grandchildren something, and transmitting knowledge and wisdom is a validating experience for all family members.

Special mission grandparents tell what they know in the spirit of describing possibilities, rather than with dogma or bigotry. Their telling for the future is a sublime creative act, which expresses facts and ideas that may or may not be heard.

Gaining a past made Mercedes, Henrique, Laura, and Keith more actively engaged with their grandchildren. Orienting their telling to the future provided Mercedes', Henrique's, Laura's, and Keith's grandchildren with more possibilities and opportunities than they had known before. Although telling the past and present for the future has inestimable worth, and increases the likelihood that grandchildren will pay attention and learn from the wisdom proffered, there are no guarantees. Special mission grandparents realize that telling makes them as productive and as constructive as they can be and that this alone brings considerable fulfillment and peace of mind.

In sum, special mission grandparents use telling as a tool to accomplish some of the following:

1. telling expresses family and community truths that have been learned through hearing and seeing;

2. telling activates and energizes family and community relationships;

3. telling changes relationships, values, and goals, and can influence the future beyond your lifetime;

4. telling corrects distortions and lies, and allows family and community issues to be discussed openly;

5. telling is a concrete action that predictably breaks through passivity;

6. telling not only revives and reviews past family relationships, but also creates new bonds;

7. telling is a dynamic starting point or launching pad for becoming a special mission grandparent;

8. telling is a powerful strategy that must be used only with care and caution;

9. telling is a lighthearted, open-minded way to communicate truths, rather than prejudiced or bigoted communications;

10. telling increases meaning, purpose, and direction in compelling ways.

Now that different starting points for becoming a special mission grandparent have been discussed, being a special agent in different kinds of families will be explored. Although diverse family conditions may appear to be in stark contrast to each other, some common denominators in special mission grandparenting experiences can be found among balanced families, traditional families, families in conflict, dysfunctional families, distant families, fragmented families, and blended families. The next chapters describe each of these different kinds of families and suggest ways in which special mission grandparents can bring about beneficial changes.

II

BEING A SPECIAL AGENT

6

Balanced Families

Special mission grandparents work towards the ideal of creating a balanced family. Balanced families have open, vibrant relationships that are based on meaningful, fluid exchanges among their members. Thus family bonds in balanced families are flexible but enduring, and relatives interact freely and easily both between genders and between generations. Balanced families are egalitarian in spirit, and relatives remain in contact with each other over time, whatever their immediate or long-term circumstances are.

In order to survive and thrive, balanced families respond effectively to ongoing social changes. Members of balanced families maintain vital connections with communities as well as with each other, and because balanced families are calm, understanding, and supportive, they are able to launch their adults and children into constructive roles in society. This means that balanced families both meet the personal needs of family members and help to build strong communities.

Balanced families continuously create and re-create conditions that enable and encourage their members to be autonomous whatever their ages and whatever their relationships to each other. Although balanced families are an ideal that does not actually exist, the varied characteristics of balanced families are found in well-functioning families. Therefore, balanced families are neither totally abstract nor removed from reality, but rather are an imagined or hypothetical whole that is made up of actual behavior patterns. A major advantage of balanced families is the fact that their members interact in ways which strengthen them. As a result, these individuals are sufficiently free to make their greatest and most meaningful contributions to others.

The diverse experiences of Craig, Pino, Cherelyn, and Betsy show how balanced families interact in different ways. Patterns of exchanges in balanced families frequently contrast with conventional family traditions, and the shared primary benefit of belonging to a balanced family is that individual needs are met so satisfactorily that their members necessarily take constructive action in a wide variety of social settings.

Although the financial, educational, and racial characteristics of Craig, Pino, Cherelyn, and Betsy differ, there are distinct similarities in their behavior. The grandparenting styles of Craig, Pino, Cherelyn, and Betsy empower them and their grandchildren, and even though they have not consciously adopted a special mission as grandparents, the balanced relationships they have helped to build in their families and communities are models for other grandparents to emulate. Relationship patterns in the families of Craig, Pino, Cherelyn, and Betsy are also goals for other grandparents to achieve, because these patterns ultimately balance families with overly rigid traditions, unnecessary conflicts, dysfunctions, or emotional distance, as well as fragmented and ineffectively blended families.

A closer look at the families of Craig, Pino, Cherelyn and Betsy shows how specific family patterns have a powerful impact on the lives of family members. Thus the quality of personal relationships influences how individuals grandparent and how they interact in their communities. Even though the families of Craig, Pino, Cherelyn,, and Betsy are separate and distinctive in their own right, there are important similarities in the ways in which their relationships are built and sustained.

Craig and Pino have lived together for twenty-two years. Craig was married for five years before his intimate relationship with Pino began, and he has two adult children and three grandchildren from this marriage. Although Pino never married, he consistently shared in grandparenting Craig's three grandchildren since their birth. Pino also has several great-nephews and great-nieces in his own family whom he grandparents. Both Craig's family and Pino's family encourage them to build relationships with their youngsters, so Craig and Pino are able to spend a great deal of time with their grandchildren and substitute grandchildren.

Cherelyn has been widowed for eight years. She travels frequently to her two sons' homes, where she helps to look after her two grandchildren. Although the primary care of both of her grandchildren is squarely in the hands of the children's parents and their regular baby-sitters, Cherelyn enjoys having this direct access to her grandchildren. She also takes her grandchildren on vacations and occasionally has her grandchildren stay with her in her home. Cherelyn's family appreciates the help and rich learning experiences she gives to her grandchildren, and they are flexible and cooperative when they make arrangements for these trips.

Betsy is a divorced professional woman who has one granddaughter. It is many years since her divorce, and she has worked hard to develop a successful legal career. Each summer Betsy travels out of state to visit her granddaughter, and she frequently includes her in her international travels—as well as in her visits to other family members—whenever she can. Betsy's family values her involvement with her granddaughter and tries to make her overnight stays enjoyable. At the same time, her relatives respect Betsy's professional achievements, and they support her wish to sustain an active career as long as possible.

Craig, Pino, Cherelyn, and Betsy enjoy their experiences of grandparenting as well as take their grandparenting responsibilities seriously. In spite of their different situations, they have some similar reactions and thoughts. Their families also appreciate their grandparenting contributions.

"My relationship with Pino is my highest priority," says Craig, "but I also care deeply about my three grandchildren. I want them to benefit from the same kind of freedoms that I have had, and more."

"Craig shares his family generously with me," says Pino. "I think passing on what we have learned in life to these youngsters makes a significant difference for the future. I try to do this in as many interesting ways as I can."

"I always include my grandchildren in my holiday plans," says Cherelyn. "However, I often take just one grandchild with me when I travel, because this helps me get to know a particular child better."

"I try to meet my granddaughter's needs whenever I can," says Betsy, "but I also get quite carried away with my legal projects. I put in as much time as I can with grandparenting, but it is important for me to continue to work professionally for as long as I can. My granddaughter learns a great deal from seeing me practice law, and I know that this will help her to have a rewarding career of her own someday."

Craig, Pino, Cherelyn, and Betsy have meaningful ongoing relationships with most members of their respective families. They are on amicable terms with their adult children, as well as with their adult nieces and nephews, and they each feel responsible for the well-being and education of their grandchildren—or great-nieces and great-nephews—in some respects. Craig, Pino, Cherelyn, and Betsy also pursue careers or community activities in their own right, which makes them strong examples for these children. Even though their grandchildren may not ever participate in the same projects, they will take themselves more seriously and get more involved with some issue or other because of what their grandparents have done with their lives. Thus the influence of elders has a powerful impact on succeeding generations.

Like Craig, Pino, Cherelyn, and Betsy, special mission grandparents interact with their relatives in ways that balance their families and keep their relationships open. That is, they have frequent, meaningful exchanges with members of different generations and members of different genders, whatever their particular circumstances may be. In addition, like Craig, Pino, Cherelyn, and Betsy, special mission grandparents cultivate professional and community interests, so that they are continuously involved in constructive activities and change imperatives that go well beyond the immediate needs and interests of their families. Whereas Craig, Pino, Cherelyn, and Betsy have helped to keep their families in balance during long periods of time without having any conscious design or plan, special mission grandparents aim to achieve balance in their families as a primary goal. Once grandparents understand that their family responsibilities have meaning, purpose, and direction, their actions become intentional and goal-directed. Creating a balanced family is worthwhile because these conditions of openness and flexibility allow grandchildren and other family members to thrive, develop their potential, and make their most effective contributions to others.

Some of the ways grandparents create and maintain balanced families are:

1. they keep in regular contact with relatives in all the different branches of their families;
2. they work against pressures to conform to other family members' expectations so that they can be free and responsible in their actions;

3. they challenge established age and gender stereotypes in order to strengthen their autonomy;

4. they recognize that major events such as births, marriages, or deaths shake up their families, so they make extra efforts to keep communications among family members open, useful, and meaningful during these stressful periods;

5. they prevent, counteract, or decrease family problems through persisting in continuing to build supportive networks in their families and communities;

6. they grandparent consistently and frequently in order to meet their grandchildren's real needs;

7. they make a habit of building up their own individual and social strengths, so that they can be worthy examples for their grandchildren and other family or community members;

8. they encourage their grandchildren to take every opportunity to transcend their immediate circumstances, and to make long range contributions to their communities.

Although special mission grandparents cannot alone create balanced families, their contributions to family exchanges make a crucial difference to overall patterns of behavior. Families can be brought into balance when one person is willing to make changes, because shifts in one relationship trigger changes in adjoining relationships. Appealing to grandparents to accept a special mission to make changes in their families is therefore both appropriate and realistic, because one person can have a significant impact on others.

SPECIAL MISSION GRANDPARENTS AND BALANCED FAMILIES

Grandparents who have a special mission play a critical role in bringing the ideal—or even the idea—of balanced families into being. Their deep understanding of family processes enables them to contribute towards creating conditions that increase the autonomy of all family members. Furthermore, because grandparents' rich experiences of the passage of time and social change are useful sources for the creation of many different kinds of healthy broad perspectives on everyday activities, their personal and social strengths inspire other family members to empower themselves and to give to others.

Whatever the circumstances special mission grandparents face, they can at least begin to work towards establishing balanced families. Although they may not make much progress in accomplishing this goal—especially if they are members of families with problems—they can nurture constructive attitudes and actions in themselves and others, which will ultimately lead to establishing more balanced families.

Therefore, special mission grandparents are essentially grounded in the ideal, idea, and reality of balanced families. They understand that family relationships can make or break the confidence and freedom of individual family members and that coming to terms with the power of these bonds and patterns of behavior is a first step towards accomplishing their most constructive goals as grandparents.

Craig, Pino, Cherelyn, and Betsy have developed strong ties with their communities as well as with their families. Similarly, special mission grandparents not only bring their families into balance, but also balance their own activities and contributions to others through relating to their communities and their families.

Craig and Pino are active in local theater groups as well as being responsible grandparents. Because their families are not inordinately demanding of their time and energy—that is, beyond that which they willingly give—Craig and Pino engage in several serious artistic pursuits that broaden their horizons. They have each received several acting and directing awards over the years, and so they are in strategic positions to foster lively cultural exchanges among their local neighborhood groups and between these groups and theaters in fairly distant cities. At present Craig and Pino are experimenting with an international exchange group among different kinds of theaters and audiences.

As none of her relatives makes requests for financial resources, Cherelyn has decided to invest some of the money her husband left her in stocks and shares. She meets regularly with a group of friends to discuss the business possibilities of a wide variety of companies, and between them they establish priorities for investing their pooled resources. Cherelyn is much more interested in profits and business ventures now than she was as a young woman, and some of her relatives seek her out for advice about how to invest their money. Cherelyn likes this particular kind of give-and-take with her relatives, and she organizes some of her travel to check out new investment possibilities.

Betsy thrives on the attention and support her family gives her as she continues to strengthen her legal skills and refine her career successes. She is more than happy to respond to diverse family needs, but she also has strong ambitions to undertake more demanding and more comprehensive legal projects. She has become a member of a team of lawyers that undertakes research and investigative work, and she feels that this task force makes substantial contributions towards improving housing conditions in different towns and cities.

It is because Craig, Pino, Cherelyn, and Betsy are members of well-functioning families that they have sufficient emotional energy to go outside their family arenas and participate in these broad social settings. Their effectiveness in their communities is largely due to the fact that they are deeply rooted in their families and that these relationships are sufficiently elastic to allow them to go out into the world as well as to play essential parts in everyday family negotiations.

BALANCED FAMILIES AND CHANGE

Balanced families are never static because they continuously adapt to their many different environments. Therefore, balanced families both initiate changes and respond to changes in society and communities. Although it is difficult even for balanced families to thrive in negative social conditions such as racial discrimination and alienation, it is always possible for families to make a shift towards becoming more rather than less balanced.

Special mission grandparents recognize the power and limitations of family influences on individual behavior and quality of life and work towards making constructive changes in their families and communities. Also, by staying in touch with different groups outside their families, they play active roles in change processes. This momentum towards balancing their families and accomplishing broad social change takes these grandparents out of passive victim roles and destructive social situations.

When we look at the lifetime accomplishments of Craig, Pino, Cherelyn, and Betsy we see how their integrated actions help to balance their families and further social changes. For example, Craig is open about his homosexuality because family support gives him the strength and courage to deal with prejudices in many different social settings. His passionate involvement with the theater earned his relatives' respect, and he made many innovations in the arrangements and substance of popular theatrical productions.

For his part, Pino's ongoing family and community relationships also boosted the effectiveness of his contributions in theatrical circles. His interest in education increased as a result of his own individual and social empowerment, and he became an influential director and drama teacher.

Cherelyn's travels broadened her widowed existence, and she was able to develop and refine her interest in making investments. Her increased confidence and effectiveness were instrumental in getting her relatives and friends involved in investing their own limited funds. In the long run the impact of these investment activities was felt in various communities, and many women followed Cherelyn's example by taking their financial resources and situations much more seriously.

Betsy forged ahead with a successful legal career that allowed her to be a key player in improving urban housing conditions. The support her family gave her enabled her to move freely into the wider society, and her dedication to grandparenting ensured that she remained grounded in mundane family realities. Betsy did not allow ambition to cloud her good judgment, and her experience of working cooperatively with her relatives was a sound basis for her professional work in a team of lawyers.

A consideration of these links between families and social change suggests how commitment to grandparenting enhances rather than limits grandparents' community contributions. Craig, Pino, Cherelyn, and Betsy were so successful at initiating changes within and outside their families largely because of the quality of the connections they maintained with their relatives and members of their communities. The personal, meaningful tone of their openness and willingness to make creative changes made them particularly valuable members of their families and their communities. Furthermore, the balanced family communications that characterized their families ensured that there was a free flow of information and support among family members. Therefore, ultimately their highly developed sense of autonomy made it possible for them to initiate responsible creative actions in their communities as well as in their families.

Balanced families allow or encourage special mission grandparents to make their most effective contributions, and they are a goal towards which these grandparents work. When family conditions are not balanced, and a variety of family problems develops, special mission grandparents move to open up relationships between family members of different genders and different generations—a constructive change that benefits all. Initiating behavior in the direction of making this kind of change in their families produces predictable shifts in patterns of interaction, which take place whatever a family's circumstances may be. For example, when families are severely dysfunctional, moving towards balance reduces their most deep-seated problems, whether these are family abuse, drug addiction, or unproductive conflict.

In sum, special mission grandparents play a crucial role in bringing families into balance. It is largely because of this persistent effort that they are necessarily significant actors in their families and communities.

When special mission grandparents behave in ways that aim to balance their families on a daily basis, they also inevitably increase their sense of purpose and meaning in their family and community transactions. These kinds of accomplishments include:

1. deliberately linking the past and future through their present-day decision making;

2. improving the well-being of others—particularly those who are disadvantaged—as well as increasing opportunities for their own grandchildren;

3. working towards building balanced families that will ensure a better future through strengthening families and communities.

Although Craig, Pino, Cherelyn, and Betsy are not as conscious of what their goals as special mission grandparents are, they helped to create and continue to maintain their own balanced families and communities through mature exchanges with their relatives and community members. Their grandparenting keeps their family relationships open, and their involvement in different communities broadens the bases of their security. Thus the achievements of Craig, Pino, Cherelyn, and Betsy inspire other grandparents to do the same, including those grandparents who are particularly embroiled in difficult or unfortunate family situations.

The following chapters describe commonly experienced family problems and how families with these problems benefit from special mission grandparents' actions for their families to become more balanced. The blocks and opportunities of traditional families, families in conflict, dysfunctional families, distant families, fragmented families, and blended families are considered, and particular attention is paid to how special mission grandparents can bring about the kinds of constructive changes that promote family and community balance.

7

Traditional Families

Traditional families are conventional in that they largely conform to middle-class standards, expectations, and patterns of behavior that have been passed down through the generations. Traditional families are usually what people have in mind when they describe a particular family as "normal," in spite of the fact that there are actually many diverse cultural traditions that families may choose to honor through their ways of relating to each other.

On the surface of things, traditional families appear to be doing well. They are orderly, with neatly defined roles based on age and sex. Furthermore, individual members of traditional families know what is expected of them, and there is a degree of certainty as well as clarity about being a member of a traditional family. Having a strong sense of belonging to the past in the present is comforting. Even though many traditional families cut themselves off from what is actually going on in wider society by identifying closely with their past family customs, this does not seem to matter when compared with the strong sense of security that is derived from being a member of a traditional family.

Thus the very familiarity of traditional families has meaning for both their members and their observers. Traditional families are indisputable proof that established values live on in the present. However, because traditional families are based on dreams or myths of the past rather than current realities, they develop their own sets of problems. Looking backwards to what is thought of as a golden age makes them less responsive to contemporary changes and less supportive or understanding of their younger generations' current needs and dilemmas.

In order to assess the liabilities and opportunities of grandparenting in traditional families, some general concerns must be addressed. Can past-oriented families really be healthy? Is there inevitably a misfit between ongoing social conditions and behavior patterns that were established in the past? How can some of the problems and disadvantages of traditional families be tackled by special mission grandparents? This chapter explores these issues.

Even though in reality traditional families express different cultures and values, they have some important shared characteristics. For example, because age and sex roles in traditional families derive from former behavior and expectations, these families tend to be hierarchical and rigid in the ways they conduct their daily routines. Older family members have more power and resources than young family members in traditional families, and men have more authority than women. However, given the many recent changes in most modern industrial societies, all kinds of relationships are moving in a direction of becoming more egalitarian. Also, contemporary ideals of companionship and personal commitments require that men and women at least think of each other as equally worthy of respect and attention. Although clearly equality between people of different ages and different genders has by no means been achieved, many people can no longer revere or live comfortably with ideals of dominance and subordination for their personal relationships.

In addition to traditional families' support for continued inequalities around sex and age, and a continued polarization of complementary gender roles, traditional families tend to be rigid and unable to adapt to contemporary changes because they are based on past expectations. Interestingly enough, the resistance of traditional families to contemporary changes is often mistakenly thought of as a strength. However, in reality this kind of rigidity decreases the likelihood that traditional families will be able to establish meaningful continuities in their family bonds in the future.

Femi, Dexter, Hugh, and Edna belong to traditional families, but as special mission grandparents they are working towards changing some of these rather suffocating conditions for themselves, their grandchildren, and other relatives. Femi and Dexter have lived together for thirty-one years, and they are still inclined to want to enact conventional family roles and expectations in their grandparenting. Hugh never married or had a long-standing personal relationship, but his life as a bachelor has been enlivened by his many nephews and nieces, and now by his grand-nephews and grand-nieces. Edna is widowed and had great difficulty in claiming her independence after many years of obedience and subservience to conventional expectations for her age, gender, and marital status.

Femi and Dexter want to have a positive impact on their grandchildren, and they think that they are more likely to accomplish this if they can change some of the conditions and limitations that have been honored through the generations by their respective families. Femi is committed to making her family's gender stereotypes less restrictive and more realistic, and Dexter wants to break down some of the rigidities in the hierarchy of control in his family.

Hugh believes that he did not marry and have a family of his own because his view of marriage was very negative. He thought marriage would hold him back from pursuing his professional and avocational interests, so he avoided becoming involved in personal relationships as a young man. However, now he wants to be more positive and more supportive about marriage and intimate relationships for his grand-nephews and grand-nieces, so that they will feel freer to make personal commitments than he did. Hugh also wants his grand-nieces and grand-nephews who want to be single to have a more rewarding emotional life than he has had.

Edna's special mission as a grandparent includes encouraging her grandchildren to learn how to be independent at very young ages. She is disillusioned about the health or wisdom of conventional family roles that require individuals to adapt to each other rather than to express themselves in their own right. Edna feels that she would have been more satisfied with her marriage—and even with being a widow—if she had known how to create and sustain these freedoms for herself.

When we consider what Femi, Dexter, Hugh, and Edna think about their own grandparenting behavior, we get a clearer view of how grandparents can work towards making constructive changes in traditional families. Traditional families can be opened up by the actions of a special mission grandparent, and changing the relationship patterns in these families gradually brings them into balance.

"I am astounded at how my relatives think about what women and men should be doing with their lives," says Femi. "There is so much wasted talent and skill in my family because my relatives coerce people into cramped roles."

Dexter expresses his dissatisfaction with the hierarchy in his family. "We have a chain of command that has been passed down for generations," he says. "It's amazing to me that my family still allows this kind of abuse to continue. We have to get beyond worshiping our pecking order if our grandchildren are to have a better future."

"In some respects I would like to live my life over," says Hugh ruefully. "I don't know why I couldn't get more with it and build a solid relationship with someone over the years, because I would certainly enjoy having a companion now. However, I'll do what I can to make this more possible for the youngsters in my family."

Edna is happy that she finally woke up to the advantages and pleasure of being independent within her family. "I have spent too much of my life ignoring or denying my own preferences and goals," she says, "so I am not willing to do this anymore. The best part of it is that my mistakes help my grandchildren because I take this freedom business very seriously now."

Although Femi, Dexter, Hugh, and Edna have many difficult tasks ahead of them in order to achieve their preferred goals, having a special mission helps them to keep focused on making specific changes and to make progress on the issues they care about most. Developing and maintaining their motivation to make a difference in their grandchildren's lives encourages the kind of grandparenting behavior that is necessary to accomplish their goals.

Special mission grandparents in traditional families are confronted with some or all of the following problems:

1. ritualized patterns of family interaction that are difficult to change;
2. intense collective resistance to individual efforts to open up family relationships;
3. powerful age and gender stereotypes that influence family members' assumptions, expectations, and behavior;
4. strong pressures to conform to family members' shared standards and values;
5. extreme polarization around different age and gender roles;

6. a rigid hierarchical ordering of family statuses where men and older family members dominate, and women and younger relatives defer to their power and authority;

7. repetitive behavior and a controlled emotional climate that inhibit the free expression and creativity of grandchildren and other family members.

Although traditional families are often lauded for being intact, the degree of their togetherness is so compelling that family members' relationships and actions are limited by relatives' disapproval or approval. Special mission grandparents pioneer in freeing up these stagnant relationships, so that their grandchildren thrive more productively.

Femi was dismayed by her family elders' views of acceptable behavior for women and men. However, she became more hopeful when she realized that she can correct some of these distortions, so that her grandchildren will benefit.

Rather than wallow in his distaste for his family's hierarchy of age and gender, Dexter decided to do what he could to interact in more egalitarian ways with as many different members of his family as possible. He knows that destabilizing his family's chain of command will enable his grandchildren to be more accepted in their own right.

Hugh uses humor to demystify his family's myths about marriage, personal relationships, and being single. He also tries to understand what it takes to make a deep, meaningful personal commitment, and he engages his grand-nieces and grand-nephews in conversations about building solid relationships. He does not wait until his grand-nieces and grand-nephews are adolescents before he raises these topics, but rather he discusses aspects of making commitments with them at very young ages.

When Edna saw how her shyness and quiet acceptance of her lot in life had impeded her development as a whole person, she started to challenge relatives who wanted to keep her in the role of a subservient widow. She has become a much more exuberant person who delights in her grandchidren, and she helps them to come into their own regardless of what other relatives think.

Thus Femi, Dexter, Hugh, and Edna begin their long journey to make the conditions in their traditional families more hospitable for their grandchildren, grand-nieces, and grand-nephews. They recognize some of the hazards and pitfalls they are faced with in their traditional families, and their efforts to make changes move them and others towards building more open and more flexible relationships.

SPECIAL MISSION GRANDPARENTS AND TRADITIONAL FAMILIES

One of the first discouraging reactions special mission grandparents have when they try to make changes in traditional families is that their individual efforts seem to be up against the insurmountable weight of all their living and deceased relatives and all their community and socially acceptable ways of doing things. This is truly a David and Goliath situation, where the odds for defining themselves successfully in light of the influence of tradition seem extremely unlikely and hazardous.

However, becoming more objective about traditional families broadens the vision of grandparents and increases their possibilities for having an impact on these powerful, established patterns of behavior. After all, traditional families are just one kind of family with its own particular problems. Bringing traditional families into balance is therefore no more or no less than bringing other kinds of imbalanced families into balance. The distinctive character of special mission grandparents is that they are strongly motivated to persist in their efforts to accomplish change in their families and that they continue to do this in spite of their families' different kinds of resistance.

Femi and Dexter were quite committed to changing gender stereotypes and patterns of dominance in their respective traditional families. Through telling her grandchildren family stories Femi was able to bring some of her women family members out of obscurity and to show her granddaughters what women had managed to accomplish in their family in spite of their subservience. Femi was also able to convince her grandsons that they can make their way in the world without impinging on the freedoms of their sisters, wives, or other women relatives. For his part, Dexter did a good job of democratizing his family's decision making, thereby increasing the autonomy of his grandchildren. Femi's and Dexter's grandchildren benefitted from these different kinds of changes in their extended kin, and at the same time they continued to be well supported by their family.

Hugh became a maverick in his traditional family. He no longer behaved predictably, and he no longer fitted into his marginal bachelor role. His outrageousness loosened up rigidities in his family, and he was successful in destabilizing his relatives' established behavior patterns, which provided new opportunities for his grand-nieces and grand-nephews. He played his grandparent role with verve, and even though he shook up his relationships with his brothers and sisters, he continued to be on good terms with his relatives, and therefore to have direct access to members of the youngest generation.

Edna concentrated first on becoming increasingly independent in her traditional family. She knew that she would be a more effective grandparent if she seized her own freedom and refused to be pushed into roles and tasks she did not want to perform. Buying a car, renting a house, taking a part-time job, and attending classes at a local college were all beginnings of her newfound independence, and these moves inspired her to create opportunities for the growth and maturation of her grandchildren's individuality and uniqueness.

TRADITIONAL FAMILIES AND CHANGE

Once special mission grandparents such as Femi, Dexter, Hugh, or Edna set these kinds of initiatives in motion in their traditional families, the entire kin group started to change. Shifting or destabilizing family rituals or stereotypes opened up relationships in traditional families, and in due course they became more balanced, more democratic, and more egalitarian. These kinds of gradual changes increase the number of opportunities available to members of the youngest generation for their own free development.

For example, Femi found that as a result of her interventions to reduce the power of distorted gender stereotypes in her traditional family, her grandchildren not only had more flexibility in making decisions about what they want to do with their lives, but they also moved out into the world with more realistic expectations for themselves. This means that whatever the social setting they find themselves in, they become valued contributors to the tasks at hand.

After Dexter took steps to reduce the influence of the established hierarchy in his traditional family, his grandchildren became more autonomous. Furthermore, they not only took advantage of the ways in which they were now able to exercise their freedom in their family, but they were also inspired to restructure and reorganize some of the community groups in which they participated. Although Dexter's grandchildren continued to respect seniority and authority in their family and in the community, they bestowed equal worth on those with whom they interacted in varied social settings and in their thinking about the needs of others and their own long-range goals.

Hugh's comic critique of his traditional family's stubborn ways led his grand-nieces and grand-nephews to develop their own strong sense of humor, which served them well in different resistant or difficult situations. Hugh's grand-nieces and grand-nephews learned to expect the unpredictable, and they were extremely creative in their diverse community ventures.

Their family bonds remained strong but elastic, and they were able to make committed personal relationships as desired.

Edna's newfound independent ways showed her grandchildren how to be brave pioneers in undertaking different vocations and community roles. Their strong sense of autonomy helped them to hold their own in routine and problematic community exchanges, and they persevered to accomplish their goals. Edna's grandchildren remained in contact with their traditional families, but their posture to their relatives, colleagues, and friends was that of innovator, discoverer, and solver of problems rather than that of people pleaser or adaptive participant.

Therefore, special mission grandparents have a responsibility to set these kinds of changes in motion in their families and in their communities, no matter how resistant their families may be. Traditional families are among the families most resistant to change because their standards and expectations frequently overlap with those of a particular group or class in society. Thus because traditional families do not stand alone, they exercise what is experienced as a buttressed authority over their members, and this is often felt to be an insurmountable barrier to change.

Grandparents learn both to expect resistance from their traditional families and to persevere in their interventions and initiatives. They know that if they persist in pursuing their goals in spite of the emotional opposition or sabotage of their other family members, their grandchildren will benefit from the changes they are making. Although their special missions cannot be completed in their own lifetimes, it is their transcendence of current problems—which comes from working towards impossible ideals—that empowers them and influences members of younger generations.

Special mission grandparents do not necessarily break down all their family traditions, but only those that restrict some or all of their family members. Furthermore, their task in accomplishing change is more in the nature of building new, healthy traditions rather than developing a free-for-all where each family member has to fend for survival.

The particular opportunities and accomplishments of special mission grandparents in traditional families vary widely but include some or all of the following:

1. grandchildren gain more autonomy and consequently develop more of their unique potential;

2. rigid ways of doing things become more relaxed, which encourages more creative action by grandchildren and other relatives;

3. hierarchical ordering in family exchanges becomes more egalitarian, with the result that exchanges are more meaningful and more genuinely respectful of each person;

4. hidden agendas to maintain the status quo become more open, and relatives work together to ensure that their growing children have supportive environments;

5. grandparents' participation in communities inspires their grandchildren to be concerned about issues and goals that go beyond honoring their own rather insular family traditions;

6. members of traditional families at all generational levels begin to establish new, more viable traditions that keep relationships both flexible and durable;

7. grandparents in traditional families deliberately combine selected values from the past in their present-day decision making, so that what they consider worth preserving will continue in the present and in the future.

Through hearing, seeing, and telling special mission grandparents formulate and communicate their beliefs and strategies about traditional families to their grandchildren and other family members. The grandparenting successes of Femi, Dexter, Hugh, and Edna were in part due to their willingness to recognize that things could be better in their traditional families and to their inclinations to experiment with a wide range of strategies of being and doing. Family traditions were changed through their initiatives, and their grandchildren, grand-nieces, and grand-nephews began to live in ways that strengthen their families and communities in the current and next generations.

8

Families in Conflict

Families should not avoid conflicts, but rather ensure that the conflicts they have are articulated clearly and are resolved as quickly and as effectively as possible. Families who deny their conflicts stagnate, splinter, and have members who grow emotionally distant from each other. Therefore, in the best of all worlds conflicts are a sign of the dynamism of families. Furthermore, the shifts in routine ways of relating that characterize conflicts enable these families to restructure themselves.

It is families in a state of perpetual unproductive conflict, which never gets resolved, that we consider here. These are the families that suffer the most negative consequences from conflict. What can special mission grandparents do if their family conflicts continue endlessly and unproductively? Although these grandparents have a constructive impact on whatever kind of family they are in, specific situations and tasks challenge them in conflicted families.

One of the most pervasive and most pernicious family conflicts that develops is that between parents and grandparents. When conflicts between parents and grandparents are not resolved, grandchildren suffer, in part because grandparents' access to them is frequently limited or curtailed by the parents who are feuding with the grandparents. Conflicts and their resulting emotional estrangements between the nuclear family of parents and children and the grandparents eventually inhibit the development of the children and limit their future well-being.

Therefore, it is very important for special mission grandparents to resolve their conflicts with their adult children and their children's spouses if they are to be effective as grandparents. This not only improves grandparents' access to their grandchildren, but it also enhances the emotional climate of all family exchanges. The link between parents and grandparents is powerful and often dominates the whole family, so unless this bond is viable, the family will break down.

In spite of the many seeming disadvantages of being a special mission grandparent in a conflicted family, there are some interesting and useful advantages. Families in conflict have a certain fluidity in that they are not static or rigid, but rather reactive and volatile. Also, whereas conflicts may break some tenuous family relationships, other family bonds are strengthened because of the conflicts. In fact, emotionally speaking, conflict is a bonding mechanism that may perpetuate more relationships than it destroys.

Guita, Luis, Kim, and Stephen are all members of conflictual families. Guita and Luis are from two tempestuous families, and their own relationship quickly became intense from their regular fights. Kim cannot remember when her family was ever calm, and Stephen is afraid of remarrying because his own family is in turmoil so much of the time.

Guita and Luis wonder how they have managed to stay together after all these years, and they prize their grandchildren. From time to time their adult children get angry with them, sometimes for no apparent reason, and they forbid either Guita or Luis—or both of them—to visit them and their children. Therefore, Guita and Luis often feel helpless as grandparents, because their children manipulate their relationship with their grandchildren in a never-ending sequence of extraordinary ways.

Kim is afraid of her brother, and the fact that they have been estranged over the years has not helped her to have a healthy relationship with her adult children. Stress in her relationship with her brother has affected and still affects her ability to parent autonomously, and she lacks confidence to be the kind of grandparent she really wants to be. Kim's children do not respect Kim for allowing this unresolved conflict with her brother to continue, and they sometimes do not let Kim see her grandchildren.

Stephen is still so caught up in a conflict he had with his father as a boy, which he never managed to resolve, that he is not interested in being a grandparent. He ignores the needs of his adult children and his grandchildren because he does not want to stir up old memories of how he suffered as a child through conflicts with his arrogant and domineering father. Being unable to let go of the past, Stephen cannot be effective in the present and the future.

"All I want is a peaceful family life," says Guita, "but there never seems to be an end to the battles we fight. We don't get anywhere by ranting and raving, and I dread to think what effect these fights have on our grandchildren."

"Just because my own family fought all the time does not mean that I have to continue the fight in my own family," says Luis. "I wish I could take charge of my life so that I don't have to disagree with my grown children all the time. I can't enjoy grandparenting while all this is going on!"

"If only my brother and I could be friends," laments Kim, "my children would respect me, and I would be able to be a better grandparent. I have not even tried to make it up with my brother, because I am not sure why we are fighting in the first place. I hope I will find out how to stop this conflict before it reaches my grandchildren."

"It has taken me a long time to realize that I don't like being with my family because of the clashes I had with my father," says Stephen. "I did not think that our disputes could be carried into the present and future, especially not after my father's death, but I never seem to get away from the issues we fought about. I hope this conflict won't follow me to the grave, and that my grandchildren will not suffer because of this conflict."

Even though Guita, Luis, Kim, and Stephen have some idea about why there is conflict in their families, they have to pinpoint the issues they really care about before they will be able to put their unproductive conflicts aside and go on with their lives. Having a new focus as special mission grandparents helps to pull them out of their unnecessary and unproductive conflicts. Developing a special mission requires energy and attention and makes it more difficult to divert energy to old conflicts.

Guita and Luis welcome their special mission as grandparents as a way to create a breathing space amidst their perpetual conflicts. Considering what her special mission as a grandparent might be allowed Kim to form a healthier perspective on her relationship with her brother, because she had to decide which grandparenting goals she really wanted to pursue. Even Stephen responded positively to the idea of having a special mission as a grandparent. He began to let go of the past a little by believing that he had important present and future projects to work for, and he became somewhat interested in starting to build relationships with his grandchildren.

Thus although these serious family conflicts did not disappear overnight, they became more manageable or more tolerable because Guita, Luis, Kim, and Stephen began to plan constructively for the future. When they took charge of their lives and their out-of-control conflicts by making decisions about what they wanted to do for their grandchildren, the power these conflicts had over them began to subside.

Some of the characteristics and hazards of families in conflict for special mission grandparents include:

1. the intensity of conflicts that have been passed down through the generations may be so strong that they are experienced as self-perpetuating and impossible to change;

2. grandparents who are afraid to get angry do not want to try to resolve their family conflicts, especially those long-standing conflicts that seem to have no real reason to exist in the first place;

3. because grandparents may not have had any success in resolving conflicts, they are reluctant to tackle or make inroads on conflicts that dominate all their family exchanges;

4. grandparents may fear losing even their limited access to their grandchildren if they face up to some of the unresolved conflicts with their adult children;

5. family conflicts are merely recycled rather than resolved if grandparents are not sufficiently committed to getting rid of the worst effects of their long-standing family differences;

6. because family conflicts are multifaceted, and involve and affect many family members, grandparents may find it difficult to believe that one person's actions can make such a difference that resolution will ultimately follow;

7. family conflicts that are not played out by the usual feuding parties may move around a family relationship system, so that other family members express these same tensions;

8. grandparents may not be able to concentrate sufficiently to design their own agendas, due to the intensity of ongoing family conflicts;

9. some family conflicts—for example, between a parent and a grandparent—may protect grandchildren, in that many differences are fought out at generational levels that are removed from their grandchildren;

10. it is sometimes difficult to distinguish productive conflicts from unproductive conflicts, so patterns that work towards family stagnation rather than family renewal may be perpetuated.

Ideally special mission grandparents set out on a track that leads them to understand the nature of their family conflicts and their many complex manifestations. It is in part this understanding that convinces them to start to change their own behavior in relation to the conflicts. Above all, having a special mission allows grandparents to transcend their ongoing family conflicts and to become immune to conflicts' emotional demands of allegiance and fear. Furthermore, because special mission grandparents become more objective about their family conflicts, they are more likely to be able to begin to resolve them than if they remain immersed in this unproductive drain of energy and motivation.

SPECIAL MISSION GRANDPARENTS AND FAMILIES IN CONFLICT

Guita, Luis, Kim, and Stephen each started to face up to the damage that conflict was doing in their families. Guita refused to enter into the kinds of fights that she had helped to perpetuate over the years, and she concentrated more on what she could do to develop her grandchildren's different interests and inclinations. When she made it clear to her relatives that she was not going to fight as usual, some of the conflicts subsided or shifted between other family members. Guita made sure that she tried to reach some agreements or understanding with her adult children, and although this was not possible in the short run, she persevered in making these intentions known for the long haul.

Luis also diverted his attention to being a more committed grandparent rather than continuing to participate in established family conflicts. He was more confrontational in his style of trying to resolve conflicts than Guita, but he too made it clear to his relatives that he was not going to fight the old fights. His orientation to the future strengthened, and he tried to plan with his adult children for the education and welfare of his grandchildren.

Kim decided to seek counseling help to resolve the long-standing tensions with her brother. She was not confident that approaching her brother directly would work, but when she did this they both decided that there had been enough hurt from their differences and that they would start to relate more openly as equals. Kim told her brother that she wanted to do what is best for her grandchildren, and he agreed that everyone would benefit from their getting along better. Kim's adult children were proud that their mother had finally taken this initiative, and they became much more relaxed about letting Kim have access to her grandchildren.

Stephen also decided to seek outside help to get over his life-long conflict with his father. His group therapy supported his ventures to get to know his father better, even through his death, and Stephen began to let go of his past hurts sufficiently so that his present behavior changed. He was much more able to express his affection to his children and grandchildren, and he wanted to start his individual quest to be a special mission grandparent.

Like Guita, Luis, Kim, and Stephen, grandparents who want to develop a special mission must take some initiatives to reduce the conflicts in their families. Even as relative bystanders, they have some responsibility for the perpetuation of unproductive conflicts in their families, and they have to halt their implicit approval or participation in these destructive patterns. Although each individual has to see the specificity of the conflicts clearly in order to work out effective strategies, being direct and honest is a first necessary step towards resolving these kinds of difficulties. A further responsibility of special mission grandparents is to see that conflicts are not merely disguised, so that they reappear. Genuinely peaceful and respectful exchanges have to be maintained through time, so that all family members can be sufficiently confident to go forward with their own plans for personal development and community contributions.

When Guita saw that the conflicts in her family had subsided, she started to take her grandchildren to Spanish-speaking cultural events, so that they could learn more about their family culture. Reducing conflict in his family enabled Luis to see that he wanted to introduce his grandchildren to athletics. He was able to spend much time coaching them and attending their meets, so that he could cheer them on in their sprinting and long-distance running events.

Kim was much relieved to find that her renewed relationship with her brother gave her the confidence to relate more openly with her adult children. She busied herself with Chinese cooking and brought food she had prepared to family picnics and reunions. She taught her grandchildren to help her to cook, and they learned about their family's history as they worked along with Kim.

Stephen was able to write more easily as he resolved his past conflict with his father. He had always wanted to be a journalist as a young man, and although this dream could not be fulfilled, he got great satisfaction from teaching his grandchildren how to write journals and stories. He encouraged them to take themselves seriously, and he read some of what he had written to them. These activities strengthened his bonds with his children as well as with his grandchildren, and Stephen vowed to continue to resolve his relationship with his father at every opportunity.

FAMILIES IN CONFLICT AND CHANGE

The initiatives special mission grandparents take to resolve conflicts in their families change the dynamics among their relatives and free up their grandchildren to be themselves and to pursue their own interests. When their family conflicts are reduced, these grandparents and other relatives can think through what kinds of contributions they want to make to their communities and act accordingly. Thus special mission grandparents start a cycle of change in their families that otherwise lies dormant or is suppressed because family members' energy goes into the conflicts.

Conflicted families are inevitably cut off from their communities. They are also in a state of perpetual unproductive motion, where they spin their wheels aimlessly. This isolation of families in conflict is not conducive to supporting their members to make community contributions, and it drains their inclinations to make moves outside their families. It is only when family conflicts are sufficiently reduced that family members can develop their potential and give to others.

As community contributions accomplish change and bring about the betterment of society, members of families in conflict can not play critical roles in making changes. Only when special mission grandparents, or other motivated family members, work towards reducing the habitual conflicts can relatives participate in broader change processes.

It took some time of actively trying to reduce conflict in her family before Guita even learned about cultural events in the Spanish-speaking section of her town. As her family conflicts subsided, she was able to develop her interest in music, theater, and dance, and then she gradually included her grandchildren in these activities. She could only concentrate on music, theater, and dance, and support them through her participation, when family conflicts no longer drained her energy.

Luis had been a competitive runner as a boy and young man, but he had not cultivated this interest through the years. When he felt that his family was beginning to calm down, he reactivated this hobby. After he retrained himself, he got his grandchildren involved, as well as some less privileged children in his neighborhood. He knew that he was sufficiently talented in athletics to be able to help these youngsters develop their potential and interests. He also encouraged his grandchildren to become responsible for helping those who are less fortunate than themselves.

Kim had been interested in Chinese cooking for many years, but she had kept her skills hidden. She gained self-confidence from resolving her conflict with her brother, and she realized that cooking was an activity she could do with her grandchildren and at family reunions. She created occasions for her relatives to get together around her cooking, and through these contacts she began to compile a family history. Both Chinese cooking and getting to know the history of their family were positive experiences for Kim's grandchildren, and as a result they broadened their perspectives.

Stephen became sufficiently freed up to pursue writing as an avocation when he found out how to resolve his conflicts with his father. Coming to terms with the past included making contacts with relatives and friends who had known his father and who had realized the issues expressed in his conflicts. When Stephen had made sufficient progress with his long-term resolution of this relationship he began to write, and later he included his grandchildren in his writing experiments. Although it was no longer possible for Stephen to become a full-time journalist, he sent freelance work to his local papers and wrote a newsletter about his former occupation as an engineer. As Stephen circulated his ideas in writing he contributed to the education of his grandchildren as well as to broader change processes.

This kind of involvement with communities allows grandparents in conflicted families to rise out of these unproductive repetitions of behavior and to contribute to social change. Guita, Luis, Kim, and Stephen broadened their horizons sufficiently so that they were no longer victims of their family conflicts, but rather they grandparented through involving their grandchildren in community life. Kim's family history also freed other relatives as well as her grandchildren, and all members of her family benefitted from the reduced daily conflicts and estrangements.

Special mission grandparents' observations about family conflicts help them to play a leading role in continuing to decrease their family conflicts. They are skilled at being open in their communications, and they try to resolve conflicts when they arise, rather than letting hurt feelings fester and estrangements develop. Some of the ways in which special mission grandparents successfully reduce family conflicts are:

1. they confront conflictual family members by telling them how their attitudes and actions affect others, especially their grandchildren;

2. they refuse to participate in family conflicts, even though they may have been key players in these conflicts in the past;

3. they resolve stressed relationships by interacting with people who are emotionally close to those who are central to the conflict;

4. they put together a historical perspective on their family conflicts and on other family activities;

5. they transcend ongoing conflicts that they have not been able to resolve by cultivating projects that connect them to their communities;

6. they support their grandchildren in finding daily solutions to dilemmas caused by others' conflicts;

7. they show their grandchildren that family conflicts are both unnecessary and a waste of time and energy;

8. they prevent the escalation of family conflicts by being open in their communications, and by expressing their differences long before they develop into full-blown conflicts;

9. they make sure that their relationships with their adult children are sound, so that they will continue to have access to their grandchildren.

Special mission grandparents can make a vital difference to the emotional climate of their families. Guita, Luis, Kim, and Stephen not only transformed their own lives by reducing the conflicts in their families, but they also improved the quality of life for all the members of their families. Their grandchildren benefitted from these changes because they could not initiate the behavior that led to the resolution of the conflicts and because they could not pursue community activities and make community contributions alone.

9

Dysfunctional Families

All families are dysfunctional in some respects, and alcohol or drug abuse, family violence, or sexual aberrations are found in many families. It is because all the members of a dysfunctional family influence the structure and intensity of a particular dysfunction that the decisions and actions of a single special mission grandparent can make a difference, and eventually reduce that dysfunction. Therefore, each family member plays a part in either creating or eliminating family dysfunctions.

Although special mission grandparents often intervene in their family problems indirectly, what they do can modify the most pernicious causes and consequences of family dysfunctions. They accomplish this by opening up flexible, extensive relationship networks within their families and communities, which reduce the tensions that originally caused the dysfunction, as well as the stresses that built up around the dysfunction.

Rob, Lorraine, Tama, and Warren were all from dysfunctional families. Rob and Lorraine were dysfunctional when they married twenty-seven years ago, in that they were both active alcoholics who came from families where alcohol abuse was widespread. Tama had a father who was a drug addict, and her brother is addicted to heroin now. Warren physically abused his wife for many years before she left him, and now he is afraid of starting another relationship because his father had also physically abused his mother, and Warren feels doomed to repeat his abusive behavior.

In spite of their dysfunctional family backgrounds, or even because of them, Rob, Lorraine, Tama, and Warren are determined to be effective grandparents. They see the opportunity to grandparent as a way to make up for some of the difficulties they had as parents, particularly for the problems they created when their children were little. Even though only Rob, Lorraine, and Warren have been dysfunctional parents, Tama knows that the problem behavior in her family has in part been sustained through her own acquiescence. She was a passive but willing participant in her family's dysfunction.

"We may never have married if we weren't a couple of drunks," says Lorraine. "I never thought, at the time, that there was anything wrong with the way we did things. We enjoyed ourselves so much!"

"There's nothing like hiding behind alcohol," says Rob. "I wonder what we would have done with our lives if we had not come from alcoholic families in the first place."

"I do not want to repeat the kind of abuse my father inflicted throughout his life," exclaims Warren. "I must make other choices about my grandchildren. They need me to be there for them."

"I have spent so much time trying to deny my involvement in our family's drug addiction problems that I have not even tried to put things right," sighed Tama. "Getting honest about my own duplicity should help to improve matters for the whole family."

Rob and Lorraine have abstained from alcohol for more than ten years. Other members of their families have also stopped drinking, and on the surface of things it appears that all is well and their families are no longer dysfunctional. However, Rob's sister and one of Lorraine's cousins have difficulty maintaining their abstinence, and they still binge on alcohol occasionally. Also, members of Rob's and Lorraine's families are very thin-skinned and reactive, so the emotional tone of family exchanges is volatile.

Tama's brother is institutionalized for his heroin problems, and with him out of sight Tama's family seems almost normal. However, her brother's drug habits have left their impact on several family members, and much anger and many hurt feelings fester around the issue of his drug addiction. Furthermore, Tama is sometimes rejected by her relatives because of her father's and her brother's drug addiction problems.

Warren intimidated his children and relatives by his brutality to his wife, and although he successfully completed a rehabilitation program, most members of his family will have nothing to do with him. Warren not only wants his relatives to forgive him for his sordid past, but he also wants to be a respected grandparent. He suspects that although it may be too late for him to make up to his adult children for his violent ways of the past, he should be able to make a fresh start with his grandchildren.

Whether special mission grandparents have dysfunctional habits themselves or not, or whether they are merely enablers for other relatives' dysfunctions, they can each relate to perpetuators and enablers in ways that reduce the seriousness of the dysfunction. Rob's and Lorraine's experiences as alcoholics allow them to recognize early signs of alcoholism in other family members. Tama's secondhand experiences of drug addiction make her sensitive to behavior that could lead to drug addiction. Similarly, Warren is adept at knowing warning signals of the onset of physical abuse in his family. Therefore, Rob, Lorraine, Tama, and Warren are not only experts in different kinds of family dysfunction, but also, with their knowledge about signs and symptoms, they can help to prevent a particular full-blown dysfunction from developing.

As they try to grandparent effectively, special mission grand-parents necessarily get involved with conditions that precipitate or perpetuate family dysfunctions. Because they want their grandchildren to benefit from not having dysfunctional fami-lies, they make moves towards eliminating the dysfunctions. The particular steps they take include opening up relationship systems in their families and building supportive networks for their grandchildren.

Thus dysfunctional families are not so set in their ways that their problematic patterns of behavior cannot be reversed. Fur-thermore, it takes only one committed family member, perhaps a special mission grandparent, to throw a spanner in the works so that the family relationship system does not continue to carry on its dysfunctional business as usual. However, taking the ini-tiative to interrupt these intense and resistant family processes requires much courage, and such acts are not easy for a special mission grandparent to perform. The payoff for making this kind of difference, however, is enormous. If the changes are maintained, the lives of grandchildren are saved and a better fu-ture assured.

The posture special mission grandparents take to family dys-functions varies, but the following characteristics are usually ap-parent:

1. they assume a measure of responsibility for the develop-ment and perpetuation of the family dysfunction;
2. they are prepared to do what they can to ameliorate the symptoms of the dysfunction, and to neutralize the original causes of the symptoms;
3. they are committed to shielding their grandchildren from the most pernicious consequences of the dysfunc-tions;

4. rather than deny the dysfunctions or hide from the effects of the dysfunctions, special mission grandparents conduct themselves openly and directly with regard to the dysfunctions;

5. they continue to build open relationships with as many relatives as possible rather than only focus on the most dysfunctional family members;

6. they continue to make meaningful connections with their communities, so that they keep their perspectives broad and maintain their unique contributions to others;

7. they concentrate on doing preventive relationship work, so that probabilities of repeating the dysfunctions are minimized;

8. they stay alert to the possibility that dysfunctions may be merely recycled or may erupt between other family members;

9. they remain satisfied if all they can do is move towards eliminating dysfunctions, as many conditions cannot be changed in a short period of time;

10. they pass on their know-how to their grandchildren, so that they can fend for themselves more effectively and avoid being caught up in any aftermath of the dysfunctional behavior of other family members.

Special mission grandparents like Rob, Lorraine, Tama, and Warren build on their own life experiences of dysfunctions and attend to the details necessary to reverse them. They understand that their actions, however minuscule they seem, will make a difference in the lives of their grandchildren, and they pursue their grandparenting objectives relentlessly. It is only through persistence that the emotional systems of family relationships can be tempered and dysfunctions reduced.

Although Rob, Lorraine, Tama, and Warren could by no means eliminate all the signs and symptoms of dysfunction in their families, they reversed the shared expectation that their grandchildren would become dysfunctional. By raising responsibility issues among their relatives, they were able to sort out the facts related to the particular dysfunctions and get some acknowledgment that these patterns were neither ordained by fate nor produced by passive victims. Seeing family relationships in relation to family dysfunctions showed how ways of relating produce harmful stresses and virulent reactions, which influence the development and timing of symptoms. For example, both Rob and Lorraine were particularly dysfunctional around the time of their marriage, as this was a stressful time for them. Tama was more supportive of her brother's drug addiction after the death of her father, and Warren was more abusive to his wife around the times she was pregnant.

SPECIAL MISSION GRANDPARENTS AND DYSFUNCTIONAL FAMILIES

Lorraine used several different strategies to reduce dysfunctions in her family. She first examined why it was that some family members had more alcohol problems than others, and then she looked at how these dysfunctional individuals were linked to other relatives in her family. She found that she and the most symptomatic family members had difficulty in holding their own in their closest emotional relationships and that when those who abused alcohol were able to exercise their initiative they became less symptomatic.

Rob looked more closely at his family's history to try to discover the roots of his alcoholism and the effect that other relatives' alcohol problems had on his own dysfunctional behavior. He saw that his family had difficulty adapting to deaths and that there was more alcohol abuse around loss than at other times.

Tama was not able to find much more drug addiction in her family than that of her father and brother, but she recognized some other ways in which her family tended towards dysfunction. Several of her relatives had been institutionalized for emotional breakdowns and mental illnesses, and some had suffered from depression. She began to think that there may be a link between the different kinds of dysfunctions in her family and that the symptoms experienced were a matter of inability to conduct one's life in a balanced way.

Warren resisted looking at the incidence of physical abuse in his family, but when he did he found several sets of suspicious circumstances like premature deaths, accidents, and poor health. Although he was not ready to link these characteristics with physical abuse, he was surprised that there seemed to be some repetitions of these kinds of behavior through the generations of his family.

Although other special mission grandparents may not want to think of current family dysfunctions in a historical context, the further back they can trace problematic behavior the more likely they will be able to find some of the originating conditions of these kinds of imbalances and disorders. At least special mission grandparents are trying—through hearing, seeing, and telling—to get a clearer sense of what the precipitating conditions of their family dysfunctions are, and as long as they remain committed to being open and direct in their communications with their relatives, some progress will be made.

Lorraine persisted in asking her relatives how they had wanted their lives to turn out. This gave her a view of how satisfied they had been with their family relationships and to what extent they had felt coerced by others to fill certain roles.

Rob proceeded to find out more details about his deceased relatives, and he discovered that many of them had been incapacitated by chronic alcoholism or other chronic complaints, so that they had not lived fully in their later years.

Tama considered the size of the families in past generations and concluded that relationships must have been estranged rather than meaningful. Many of her relatives seem to have isolated themselves from the rest of the family, and these same relatives had not done as well with their lives as those who had stayed connected.

Warren looked at the life span of some of his deceased relatives, and he found that many of them died at younger ages than would have been expected. Although he did not have many details about the circumstances of these premature deaths, he wondered whether their struggles were in some respects related to the difficulties his father and he had had in living a routine life.

Special mission grandparents therefore both keep looking for answers and stay curious about the power of family relationships in their lives. Although it is difficult to come up with concrete facts about family dysfunctions, it is possible to get to know something about the emotional climate that prompted some of these symptoms to appear.

DYSFUNCTIONAL FAMILIES AND CHANGE

When families change from being dysfunctional to functioning well, they modify not only their patterns of family interaction but also their family members' orientations and actions in their communities. Optimally functioning families have members who play significant roles in society at large as well as in their families, in that they are able to make solid contributions to others at the same time that they meet their own needs. Thus when grandparents take the lead in initiating improvements in their family's functioning, they also strengthen their contributions to outside interests and projects that express their unique talents and skills.

Dysfunctional families are blocked by problems such as alcohol abuse, drug addiction, and family violence. These symptoms drain their family members' emotional resources and their abilities to plan ahead, because almost all their energy goes into trying to survive or into reacting to whatever their dysfunctional family members are doing.

When we look at how Lorraine, Rob, Tama, and Warren came into their own as special mission grandparents, we see that their efforts followed a similar sequence of events. For example, Lorraine could not make much headway with developing any of her community interests until her relatives were able to control their drinking problems. She decided to volunteer at a halfway house for alcoholic women when she realized that she had done all she could about her family's alcoholic behavior. For his part, Rob needed his family to become more calm before he could decide what he wanted to do in his community. He decided to help in a boys' club for the children of alcoholics, because he knew that he had reliable background knowledge for this position and this work would give more opportunities to his grandsons to understand their family.

Tama and Warren had similar experiences. After Tama had made peace with her family members she decided to enroll in computer classes. She knew that this would give her strong outside interests to pursue and that she could teach her grandchildren some of these skills. After some delays in getting adjusted to his new family roles, Warren followed his heart's desire to take up painting. He was gratified that some of his relatives started to accept him as a new person.

Throughout this time Lorraine, Rob, Tama, and Warren did what they could to bring their families into balance, and in due course their family dysfunctions showed marked improvements. They also experimented with different ways to be effective grandparents and found that their grandchildren were more able to concentrate on their shared activities with them because they were less apprehensive about what was going to happen next in their families. Their family lives had become more orderly and more controllable, so that they now had healthier kinds of relationships and attitudes.

Through their successes in accomplishing small-scale changes, special mission grandparents automatically enter into the broader arenas of community and societal change. Thus they not only open up their immediate family relationships so that their family dysfunctions can be brought under control, but they also become strong examples for their grandchildren by making unique community contributions. When grandparents stop reacting to their long-standing family dysfunctions in the usual ways, they inevitably shake up their family relationships sufficiently so that they create shifts in their relatives' behavior. These families begin to focus less intently on their problems, which makes finding solutions possible, and more constructive ways of relating to each other gradually emerge. Because special mission grandparents are able to inspire their other relatives to follow suit, their individual and family symptoms subside.

There are no guarantees that all these stages of change will be achieved by special mission grandparents, but rather that this sequence of events will predictably follow when grandparents in dysfunctional families are effective in reducing the family dysfunctions and persist in building supportive family and community networks for their grandchildren. However, even these seemingly indirect approaches of grandparents make a world of difference to their families' functioning and to the kinds of community contributions that all family members can make.

The results grandparents can expect from intervening in their dysfunctional families vary according to their ability to stay in touch with the dysfunctional members or parts of their families and, at the same time, to move ahead with their own grandparenting and community goals. Although it may seem impossible to do all of these things at once, there are ways to keep these different kinds of relationships open through working towards the reduction of symptoms and dysfunctions.

Just as the results of special mission grandparents in families with dysfunctions vary, so do some of their approaches to reducing dysfunctions and to grandparenting and community involvement. Here are some of the strategies that special mission grandparents use to accomplish these goals:

1. establish and maintain meaningful contact with their most dysfunctional family members and those who are emotionally closest to them;

2. create and sustain open communications with as many of their family members as possible, so that secrets about family dysfunctions do not inhibit their attempts to balance family relationships;

3. tell their grandchildren what is going on in their family without blame or judgment;

4. pursue deliberately chosen community activities so that they do not become preoccupied with wanting to do more than they can about their family dysfunctions;

5. make habits of reviewing their progress towards reducing family dysfunctions regularly—at least each week—and of keeping track of the different kinds of changes that are being accomplished;

6. participate in major family events such as births, marriages, and deaths, and at the same time observe and intervene when dysfunctional behavior patterns emerge;

7. maintain positive attitudes towards the principles of being able to reduce family dysfunctions and of being able to make a real difference in their grandchildren's lives.

By following some or all of these strategies grandparents can at least begin to make moves in the direction of relieving their families of repeated dysfunctions. As in the families of Lorraine, Rob, Tama, and Warren there will be some progress over time as relationships come more into balance. Although there are no overnight reversals of dysfunctions, predictable sequences of events can be set in motion, so that families move towards becoming functional rather than thoughtlessly or aimlessly strengthening their dysfunctions. If no one intervenes and breaks the chains of reactions in dysfunctional families, business as usual will re-create the dysfunctions and make them even more resistant to change.

One of the important payoffs for being a special mission grandparent in a dysfunctional family is gaining peace of mind. This is accomplished in addition to the more tangible results of increasing the viability of relationships for grandchildren and other family members. When grandparents know that they are doing whatever they can to relieve the stresses and burdens of their family dysfunctions, this alone motivates them to go forwards into their communities, where they can also make a difference.

10

Distant Families

Distant families are thought of here as families whose members are emotionally distant or estranged from each other. It is important to consider the contributions special mission grandparents make in distant families, because much problem behavior flows from estrangements and emotional distance among relatives when there is no specific intervention to reduce distance in these families. For example, dropping out of school or inability to make lasting commitments may result from being brought up in an atmosphere of emotional distance.

Although many geographically distant families may also be emotionally distant, geographical distance is not synonymous with emotional distance. Furthermore, geographically scattered family members can beat the odds of becoming emotionally distant through choosing effective ways to communicate with each other in spite of their separations. It is possible for geographically distant families to remain in close emotional contact through regular family reunions, frequent visits, letters, telephone calls, E-mail, photographs, recordings, and other kinds of meaningful exchanges.

Perhaps because of today's increased travel and job mobility, many grandparents live far away from their grandchildren. Even though some grandchildren may live close by, others frequently do not. As a result, more deliberate efforts have to be made by

grandparents in order to keep in touch with their geographically distant grandchildren. This is necessary because it is fairly
easy for geographically distant families to become emotionally
distant, especially when their members have contact only at in-
frequent major events, like the death of a much-loved relative or
a wedding.

Special mission grandparents set themselves the task of reducing emotional distance in their families, in order to ensure
that their grandchildren are raised in conditions that lead to
their optimal development. One way they do this is to take actions so that geographical distance does not turn into emotional
distance. Although extreme emotional distance, or estrangement between family members, is a problem for all family members, it is particularly grandchildren who suffer from emotional
cutoffs between generations and between different branches of
a family, because their emotional development becomes more
difficult. For example, children have to struggle to be self-
confident when their parents and grandparents are estranged
from each other. Furthermore, emotional distance in a family
makes it more likely that problem behavior will be passed on
from generation to generation, as well as more likely that emotional distance will be repeated through the generations.

Eugene, Vivian, Darshini, and Lewis are grandparents and
great-aunts in emotionally distant families. Eugene comes from
a family that keeps secrets and does not express thoughts or feelings directly. Vivian and Darshini were closet lesbians for many
years and were rejected by several relatives when they decided to
tell their families about their personal commitment. Lewis's father was deaf, and this handicap increased emotional distance
among his relatives in a geographically distant family.

Eugene, Vivian, Darshini, and Lewis want to improve the
emotional tone of their family relationships, especially since
they feel at least partly responsible for the well-being of their
grandchildren, grand-nieces, and grand-nephews. They do not

want to be emotionally distant as grandparents in the ways that they had felt compelled to be as parents.

"I never really knew what was going on in my family when I was a child," says Eugene. "No one seemed to tell a straight story about who my relatives were, or what made them tick. I just thought that no one got along with anyone in families, and that my family was not an important part of my life anyway. It was not until I started having difficulties in my own personal relationships that I realized that I belonged to a problem family."

"Darshini and I were probably drawn to each other because of our intensity about commitments," says Vivian. "My relatives could not make commitments to each other that really worked, and I became obsessed with trying to maintain closeness with a partner of my own. I think that Darshini and I have done remarkably well to live together in spite of our families' inabilities to relate to each other."

"I admire the way Vivian has worked at being a good partner," says Darshini. "I am much less aware of my family than she is. I just knew that I wanted to leave my family so that I could be totally different from them. I got out at the first possible opportunity."

"I could never keep track of who was in my family when I was young," says Lewis. "We traveled around a lot, but some relatives would find us and zoom into the town we happened to be in. I never really got to know them, though. My father did not like to talk about the past, and I felt inhibited in our conversations because he was deaf and wouldn't wear a hearing aid. My mother constantly gave me messages about what my father thought, but this made me feel more like a stranger than his son."

Because Eugene, Vivian, Darshini, and Lewis experienced emotional distance as children, they have resolved to do what they can to create more congenial family environments for their grandchildren, grand-nieces, and grand-nephews than they had known. Eugene is genuinely curious about his family. Over the years he has learned bits and pieces about his past and present family members, and he wants to pass on this knowledge to his grandchildren. Vivian has spent so much time thinking about the nature of her family relationships that she wants to tell her grand-nieces and grand-nephews about what to do and what not to do when you want to be close to someone. Darshini wants to make sure that her grand-nieces and grand-nephews do not drop out of school or run away from their family when the going gets rough. Finally, Lewis wants to explore his family history with his grandchildren, so that they do not feel as though they are outsiders.

These are starting points of the special missions of Eugene, Vivian, Darshini, and Lewis. Having felt emotionally deprived in their earlier years, they feel even more determined than other grandparents or great-aunts to do what they can to reverse some of the distance in their families. However, even though their goals seem reasonable, they need to take into account the fact that distancing habits and patterns of estrangement are extremely tenacious and difficult to change, especially when they have been repeated through several generations. It is only when grandparents are strong individuals in their own right that they can hope to be able to reduce emotional distance in their families.

Some of the considerations that special mission grandparents must make before embarking on specific interventions to bridge distance and emotional estrangements in their families are singled out below. These are important because well-intentioned efforts to reduce emotional distance can backfire and harm an unbelievably wide range of family members. The following strategies ensure that grandparents are thoughtful and careful before they take action to reduce distance in their families:

1. reflect on where and why the patterns of emotional distance and estrangement have developed in your family;

2. make as complete a historical review as possible of family conditions that led to the development of distant relationships;

3. recognize how you tend to be distant in your relationships, and how you have been able to overcome these inclinations over the years;

4. plan to change your behavior in ways that would make a difference to the emotional climate of your family;

5. estimate how your grandchildren could be harmed by emotional distance in your family, such as how distant relationships impinge on their freedom or fail to support them;

6. examine whether or not the quality of intergenerational relationships has increased emotional distance in your family;

7. estimate how difficult it will be to bridge emotional distance and estrangements in your family based on the length of time these patterns have existed, the fixedness of your family's reactivity, and signs that shifts in these patterns have already occurred from time to time.

Eugene, Vivian, Darshini, and Lewis are not equally dedicated to becoming special mission grandparents or special mission great-aunts, but they each try to have at least some of these considerations in mind as they seek to improve the emotional climate of their families. Lewis is the most skeptical of the four about being able to accomplish any changes, and he prefers to continue to compile his family's history rather than make any particular interventions on behalf of his grandchildren. Dar-shini also questions the wisdom of intervening in her family, and she wants to see what progress Vivian makes before she considers any strategies for herself. By contrast, Eugene and Vivian are positive and enthusiastic about the potential of special mission grandparents to make a difference in distant families. However, they will have to temper their expectations because the possibility of being able to make marked changes in emotionally distant families in a short period of time is not great.

As in the cases of traditional families, families in conflict, and dysfunctional families, special mission grandparents in distant families need only to move in a direction of ameliorating problematic conditions in their families in order to accomplish some of their heartfelt goals. Any shift a family makes towards becoming more balanced makes a considerable difference to the well-being of their grandchildren, increases their peace of mind, and strengthens their capacities to be autonomous and independent. Given these parameters, grandparents are successful when they become sufficiently aware of the problem of emotional distance so that they do not perpetuate emotional distance in their families and can make an honest effort to reverse tendencies to create distance in their relationships.

SPECIAL MISSION GRANDPARENTS AND DISTANT FAMILIES

Eugene is thrilled to be a grandparent, and he is delighted to know more about who is in his family than at any other time in his life. He feels much more like an insider than ever before, and he wants to pass on this sense of belonging and security to his grandchildren. He includes his grandchildren in his many excursions to help him put his family's history together, and they benefit a great deal from getting to know who their relatives are. When Eugene makes a trip specially to collect information from relatives he does not know, he makes a big deal of getting acquainted with them. He finds that having a family history project gives him a reason to make contact with family members who have dropped out of circulation and, at the same time, presents an opportunity for him to involve his grandchildren with their relatives. Discussing why someone has not been in touch with the rest of the family for a long period of time gives Eugene a reliable handle on the distancing patterns in his family and how they repeat from generation to generation.

Vivian collects more in-depth details about her family members' personal relationships than Eugene, because she is most interested in the nuances in behavior that have led to estrangements or to a lack of emotional satisfaction. Vivian's grand-nieces and grand-nephews like to listen to her family stories, and Vivian gets them to think and talk about what it means to love someone or to spend a lifetime in a relationship. Although Vivian's grand-nieces and grand-nephews are still very young, she knows that they learn from her stories and questions and that these lessons are valuable, especially when they meet relatives along the way who enliven their exchanges.

Darshini is interested in finding out how it came to be that many of her family members have dropped out of school, jobs, or the family and what their reasons for doing so are. She sees herself as a dropout, although in recent years she has tried to discover what impelled her to leave her family, which necessitated reestablishing contact with her relatives. At this stage of her life Darshini can see the many advantages of staying in touch with her family, and she wants to pass these on to her grand-nieces and grand-nephews.

Lewis is very cautious about changing patterns of distance and estrangement in his family. He feels that he is only just getting to know his relatives and that the excitement of finding that particular family members actually exist, and making contact with them, is enough of a project for him to handle at present. He is joyous about meeting his newly discovered relatives, and he is eager to grandparent in the context of his ever-increasing kin group. He feels more secure as he broadens the base of his family relationships, as do his grandchildren, and at the same time—in spite of himself—he actually opens up his family relationships and reduces some of his family's emotional distance and estrangements.

Thus Eugene, Vivian, Darshini, and Lewis use some of the many approaches special mission grandparents can take in distant families. However, when bridges are successfully built to estranged or distant family members, these must be sustained if patterns of emotional distance are to be interrupted and dissolved on a lasting basis. For example, although Lewis was eager to discover who his family members are, he was less interested in maintaining relationships with these relatives. On the other hand, Eugene was so wrapped up in compiling a family history that he continued to make contact with the same newly found relatives, as well as keeping them informed about his research. He was constantly on the go with one or another aspect of this project.

Darshini and Vivian were also immersed in the details of their family explorations. Although they drew their grand-nieces and grand-nephews into their family research ventures, the scope of the contacts they actually made with their estranged relatives was not as broad as that of Eugene or Lewis. Therefore, they did not open up as many relationships as Eugene and Lewis, and progress in reducing emotional distance in their families was slower.

DISTANT FAMILIES AND CHANGE

When grandparents successfully reduce emotional distance in their families, their grandchildren and other relatives are freer to make contributions to the world outside their families. Because their energy is no longer caught up in fighting silent feuds, or in maintaining unproductive patterns of behavior, they can think through what they really want to do, and how they can meet others' needs as well as their own, and then act appropriately and effectively.

Being aware of problems of emotional distance helps grandparents to act more effectively in a variety of community situations and settings. Helping less privileged children to become self-confident, for example, is an invaluable contribution that special mission grandparents may make to transform a child's life. Developing public policies along these lines is an even more wide-ranging contribution, which may ultimately have a lasting impact on the quality of life in society at large.

Although Eugene, Vivian, Darshini, and Lewis did not originally have particular goals that went beyond improving the lives of their grandchildren, grand-nieces, and grand-nephews, in the course of becoming special mission grandparents they strengthened their interests in getting involved in their communities. This willingness to become engaged in broader projects strengthened their capacities to influence change processes.

The community contributions of Eugene, Vivian, Darshini, and Lewis show some of the ways in which this broadened outreach can be accomplished. Eugene started to teach religious school, because he had come to appreciate how much people's beliefs affect their behavior. Vivian enrolled in psychology and sociology classes and decided to start a second career in counseling because she knew that she understood many relationship issues at a deep level. Darshini participated in some local after-school programs, as well as in a special education program for children who are on probation. Lastly, Lewis became more active in the senior citizens' group he had attended for several years, where he organized some discussions around the theme of what grandparents can do to help their grandchildren.

The community initiatives of Eugene, Vivian, Darshini, and Lewis had ever-broadening impacts on others, and at the same time they were able to continue to include their grandchildren, grand-nieces, and grand-nephews in these different activities. Their grandchildren, grand-nieces, and grand-nephews benefitted from seeing how their grandparents and great-aunts lived out their commitments to family members and members of their communities, in order to bring about the kinds of changes they really believed in. The examples of Eugene, Vivian, Darshini, and Lewis were seen and learned at increasingly deep levels.

Special mission grandparents in distant families are pivotal in accomplishing significant changes that affect character formation in the next generation. Their concern with how their grandchildren use their emotions, and how they can be nurtured to cope with their feelings, makes their grandchildren freer in the long run. Once family members are unfettered by past hostilities and estrangements, they can be more truly supportive and create inventive, innovative family and community goals that give similar freedoms to others.

The particular overall accomplishment of special mission grandparents in distant families is that they are able to enhance the emotional tone of their families, so that their grandchildren are nurtured to be strong and competent, and to develop tenacious family loyalties as well as meaningful commitments to community projects. Some of the complex aspects of these successful results of decreasing emotional distance include:

1. an increased awareness of what emotional distance is, and how it is expressed in the different parts of their family networks;

2. an enhanced appreciation of the negative behavioral consequences that flow from emotional distance in family relationships;

3. sensitivity to the possibility that geographical distance between family members may easily become emotional distance;

4. the courage to do whatever is possible to make effective changes in patterns of emotional distance and estrangement in their families;

5. the ability to maintain those relationships that they managed to repair, so that these relationships do not become distant or estranged again;

6. a willingness to teach their grandchildren—through action—about the importance of having open, meaningful relationships in their family;

7. extending concern to the issue of the importance of resolving community issues, so that some considerable amount of their time and energy is spent pursuing constructive goals that will make a difference in the lives of others;

8. skills to develop their grandchildren's awareness of conditions in their communities, so that they too will be able to contribute to needs that go beyond their own family's purposes;

9. interest in preventing emotional distance in their families, so that it cannot develop into estrangements that can be carried through the generations.

In these ways grandparents bring balance to distant families and increase the likelihood that this balance will be maintained beyond their lifetimes. The pain of special mission grandparents' firsthand experiences of emotional distance in their families serves as a source of motivation to make things better for the next generation and to live out the rest of their lives in ways that show others how important emotional well-being is for families and society.

As in traditional families, families in conflict, and dysfunctional families, special mission grandparents in distant families make their own characteristic contribution to the enhancement of the well-being of all family members and all members of their communities. Thus they not only implement strategies that decrease their families' symptoms, but they also enhance relationship conditions in their families and increase their families' contributions to communities.

11

Fragmented Families

Fragmented families are families whose relationships have been cut off or terminated, so that individual members or particular branches of a family are separated from the rest. Thus the connectedness of a fragmented family is splintered, and family members do not interact together coherently as a group. Rather, fragmented families operate as a series of truncated relationships, which seem independent of the whole, as well as unattached to each other.

Many families split up due to divorces, deaths, relocations, unresolved conflicts, or breaches between the generations. These significant events and problematic conditions generate so much negative reactivity in their families that they rupture those relationships that are not sufficiently flexible to withstand the tensions.

Special mission grandparents play a significant role in fragmented families. Examining how their families have splintered in the past and present shows them which family relationships are the most damaged, and which are the most unresolved. When these grandparents make and maintain meaningful contacts with as many family members as possible, their relationships become more flexible, and they essentially build bridges between their family's fragments. Also, because of their strategic generational position, grandparents can bridge some of the

broken relationships in their families more effectively than
other relatives, especially if they themselves were not instrumental in fragmenting their families in the first place.

Hosin, Yanfu, Megan, and Gilroy are grandparents in fragmented families. Hosin and Yanfu have been married to each
other for almost thirty years. They both left their families behind in Korea in order to settle in the United States with their
parents when they were teenagers. Their parents broke away
from the older generations of their families in order to better
themselves financially. Their Korean relatives disapproved of
their parents' move, and consequently Hosin and Yanfu were
raised without the direct influence of their original families.
Hosin's and Yanfu's parents did not return to Korea for the remainder of their lives.

Megan's mother died when she was ten years old, and her father did not remarry. Megan and her father lost touch with her
mother's family after her death, and Megan's father was so estranged from his own family that Megan grew up knowing very
few of his relatives. Because Megan believed that her father was
pretty much all the family she had, she was eager to get married
and have a family of her own. She worships her children and
grandchildren, and she wants to do nothing more than to be a
good grandmother to her grandchildren.

Gilroy had several live-in relationships over the years, but he
married only once. His marriage ended in divorce, and Gilroy
was so antagonistic towards his ex-wife that he turned his back
on her and her family after his divorce. As a result, Gilroy's children and grandchildren grew up having nothing to do with his
ex-wife and her family.

Some comments made by Hosin, Yanfu, Megan, and Gilroy
show more details of the extent to which their families are fragmented. Although their special missions as grandparents have
different starting points, there are several similarities about the
kinds of issues they have to deal with in order to improve the effectiveness of their grandparenting.

"I think of myself as American," says Hosin, "but somehow this does not always ring true. I would like to know more about my relatives in Korea because I am connected to them, even though my parents never returned to Korea after they moved to the States so long ago."

"I don't know much about my Korean family. My parents were very reluctant to talk about their parents, or about their brothers and sisters," says Yanfu. "I feel that not knowing who my Korean relatives are is a great loss, and that I should do something about this before I get much older."

"The loss of my mother was unbearable," said Megan, "but becoming estranged from her family is also intolerable. I don't know why my father did this when I was so young. It certainly made it more difficult for me to adjust to the death of my mother, and then later my father's death. I don't want my grandchildren to lose out by not knowing who these people were and are."

"I don't seem to get to the other side of my hatred for my ex-wife," exclaims Gilroy, "but I don't do myself or anyone else any good by poisoning my children's minds against her. I must do something to prevent my grandchildren from suffering from this as much as my children have."

Hosin and Yanfu were not able to keep in touch with their Korean relatives over the years. Because their parents had wanted to have a completely new beginning in the United States, Hosin and Yanfu did not return to Korea to visit their relatives. As a result, Hosin and Yanfu put up with having fragmented families that did not adequately serve them, their children, or their grandchildren. Some of the negative experiences that resulted from putting up with their fragmented families included their children being divorced and their grandchildren having difficulties in school.

Megan became so dependent on her father over the years that she found it impossible for her to build meaningful relationships with other men. No one could give her the kind of skills, knowledge, and emotional support her father offered, so she quickly lost interest and retreated from new intimacies. The loss of her mother had also made it difficult for Megan to have close relationships with women, especially because most of her memories of her mother and her mother's family had blurred with time.

Gilroy's wandering life meant that he could not give rootedness or a strong sense of belonging to his children and grandchildren. His resentment about the breakup of his marriage is unyielding, and his children found it difficult to marry and settle down. Although Gilroy wants to help his grandchildren to have satisfying emotional relationships, he does not know how to begin to put the fragments of his family back together again.

Thus Hosin, Yanfu, Megan, and Gilroy show us some of the problems grandparents have when they are members of fragmented families. Developing a special mission as a grandparent helped Hosin, Yanfu, Megan, and Gilroy to become sufficiently free so that they could interact effectively with members of their communities as well as their families. Furthermore, having a goal to bring their families into balance enabled them to see more clearly how their families are fragmented, as well as to work out directions to follow in order to bridge these gaps and bring their families into balance.

Hosin and Yanfu decided to go back to Korea to track down some of their past family relationships and to meet relatives for the first time, so that they could better understand their families' origins and generational links. Megan began to search out both her mother's and father's relatives, in order to get a clearer sense of who she is in her family, and of how she could begin to put the fragments of her family back together again. For his part, Gilroy tried to resolve his animosity towards his ex-wife. He sees how his children and grandchildren have missed out by not having contact with her, and he also thinks that taking this step will improve some of their relationship problems.

Conditions in fragmented families are difficult to reverse because many family ruptures take place over several generations. The subtlety of relatives' daily or weekly exchanges either perpetuates or reverses family breakups. Although it is possible for special mission grandparents to make a real difference to shared habits and patterns of behavior in their families, change is gradual unless other family members also cooperate to bring their fragmented families into balance.

Some of the characteristics that inhibit special mission grandparents from taking action include:

1. widespread acceptance among relatives of the status quo of being members of a fragmented family;

2. apprehension about the possible fallout or conflict that occurs when grandparents take initiatives to intervene in family exchanges that perpetuate fragmenting in their families;

3. difficulty in formulating plans and strategies because of the considerable emotional strain of living in a fragmented family;

4. lack of knowledge of how grandchildren can be protected from some of the negative consequences of family fragmentation;

5. lack of awareness of the extent to which a family is fragmented;

6. insufficient information about a fragmented family's history, so that it is extremely difficult to pinpoint causes or principal players in family breakdowns;

7. inability to realize the benefits, in the long run, of building family networks that replace or neutralize ruptured family relationships.

Focusing on hearing, seeing, and telling about their families allows grandparents to be aware and informed about the effects of their actions. Special mission grandparents are more effective agents in their families because they are more deliberate in choosing ways to participate and intervene in family exchanges. They therefore learn how to start a momentum that brings their fragmented families into balance.

Hosin, Yanfu, Megan, and Gilroy are able to reflect on their own impairment from the fragmentation of their families and to resolve that they will follow particular strategies to reduce the ill effects of their fragmented families on their grandchildren. By keeping the broader picture of their families and communities in mind, they transcend their own past vulnerabilities and strengthen relationships in their families and communities.

SPECIAL MISSION GRANDPARENTS AND FRAGMENTED FAMILIES

Hosin benefitted a great deal from taking a trip to Korea to meet members of his family. Although many relatives his parents knew were long deceased, he was able to meet many of his cousins and their children. He was treated with a great deal of respect, rather than the marked disapproval his parents experienced, and he offered hospitality to relatives who showed an interest in coming to the United States.

Yanfu was disappointed to find that when she arrived in Korea, many of her relatives had moved out of the village where her parents had been born. It was discouraging for Yanfu to find that the rest of her Korean family had become fragmented, and that during her month's visit, she was not able to make contact with as many relatives as she would have liked. However, when-

ever she was successful in finding a relative, she was warmly received, in spite of having language difficulties in their
communications. When Yanfu returned to the States she started
to learn Korean, so that she could more easily return to Korea to
track down more relatives.

Megan was gratified to discover that both her mother's relatives and her father's family were pleased that she wanted to get
to know them. They responded to her telephone calls and letters by inviting her to visit, and they were gracious and interested in her quest to piece together a picture and history of her
family. One immediate benefit that Megan felt was a stronger
sense of belonging and a greater feeling of security about being
herself. Megan also knew that she would be able to pass on these
strengths to her grandchildren.

It took Gilroy some time before he started to try to locate his
ex-wife. Finally he decided to take the bull by the horns and ask
her to meet with him. After she agreed to set up a time and
place, Gilroy told her about his resentments and his wish to be
free from this emotional turmoil. His ex-wife said that she did
not harbor ill feelings about their difficult relationship and that
he should accept the fact that they had both built independent
lives since their divorce. Although this exchange was not a
cure-all for Gilroy, he had made an effective beginning in bringing balance to his family. He had also accepted the reality of his
ex-wife and their divorce in his exchanges with his grandchildren.

The most important deed grandparents can do to bring balance to fragmented families is to begin the arduous tasks necessary to rebuild their ruptured relationships. Because an end
point of completely healed broken bonds cannot be reached,
establishing a firm foundation for future initiatives is critical to
making family conditions better for their grandchildren.

Hosin, Yanfu, Megan, and Gilroy were successful in turning
their families around from becoming more fragmented to becoming more whole and more balanced. Their actions and ini-

tiatives were catalysts for setting constructive changes in motion, and they continued to work on their commitments to make a difference for their grandchildren as special mission grandparents.

Even though fragmenting processes can be reactivated by new major events such as deaths and migrations, the consequences of these shifts in family patterns will not be as severe as long as grandparents continue to keep in touch with large numbers of family members. Opening up family relationships serves as an antidote to fragmentation, and flexible bonds will stretch and continue to be viable rather than break.

FRAGMENTED FAMILIES AND CHANGE

When fragmented families come more into balance, communities are strengthened. Furthermore, family members are able to make contributions to their communities rather than use all their energy in trying to survive the pressures of being in a fragmented family.

Hosin started to participate in Korean cultural events in his community. These activities enriched his basic Korean language skills, and he made many contacts with Koreans who had immigrated to the United States. He included his grandchildren in these events and connections, and they were able to get a stronger sense of their ethnic origins. Hosin also took one grandchild on his second visit to Korea and planned to take other grandchildren on succeeding visits. He therefore set himself an agenda to become more integrated with a Korean way of life and his Korean family sources.

Yanfu started classes in Korean and included her grandchildren in her study assignments. She never tired of repeating Korean words with them, and she believed that their becoming familiar with the Korean language would help them to understand more about their family origins. As Yanfu's language skills increased, she started to write to some of her relatives in Korea, and she gathered as much information as possible about where different family members had settled, and what they are doing, since her parents left Korea. This preparation helps her to plan her next trip to Korea, as well as her succeeding visits.

Megan became so well acquainted with her mother's and father's families that she started to study family theory at a local community college. She became fascinated with how her family interacts, and she makes sure that her grandchildren know about their family heritage. Megan also helps to counsel pregnant teenagers and advises them on how to stay in touch with their families as they deal with their problems. Her experiences as a special mission grandparent help her to describe three-generation dynamics to the teenagers, and by keeping this broad picture of their families in focus, some of their estrangements are bridged.

Gilroy was greatly relieved by his calling of a truce with his former wife, and his grandchildren have become quite matter-of-fact about their grandmother. This means that the emotional intensity around his grandparenting is sufficiently freed up for him to be able to become more active in his community. Gilroy chose to participate in local politics, and he engages his grandchildren in discussing some of the most controversial issues of the day. Some of his older grandchildren also help Gilroy to organize elections, and they are more aware of differences and choices among different policies.

Thus the progress Hosin, Yanfu, Megan, and Gilroy made in becoming special mission grandparents also led to their increased participation in community affairs. They and their grandchildren were able to meet others' needs as well as their own, and their particular experiences as members of fragmented families strengthened their capacities to give to relatives and interest groups in their communities. In the long run their fragmented families became more balanced, and their grandchildren learned a great deal from the examples of Hosin, Yanfu, Megan, and Gilroy.

Other special mission grandparents can accomplish similar kinds of changes in their fragmented families and their communities. Although in some cases it will take more than a single lifetime to reverse some of the intergenerational fragmenting that has occurred, merely making a start in this process can work wonders for grandparents, grandchildren, and others. At least some temporary kinds of balance can be achieved, which lead to more constructive permanent developments.

Knowing what some of the benefits of bringing a fragmented family together are motivates grandparents to intervene in broken family bonds. Hosin, Yanfu, Megan, and Gilroy turned their fragmented families around successfully because they set processes in motion that reintegrated broken key relationships. While Hosin and Yanfu concentrated on cultural aspects of their newly established links with their Korean families, both Megan and Gilroy made more direct emotional connections with their estranged relatives. Megan and Gilroy show that even in cases of death and divorce, ongoing meaningful family bonds can be built with survivors and with those who are close to deceased relatives or former spouses. Some of the advantages of bringing fragmented families into balance include:

1. family networks become more supportive of their members because they interact as a whole rather than as independent parts;

2. deaths and divorces are grieved and overcome more effectively when close family bonds are built or reactivated to fill in relationship gaps that have been left by death or divorce;

3. intergenerational connectedness is renewed, so that breaches between generations no longer cause overloading in the emotional relationships of the families that are cut off from the whole;

4. grandchildren get a stronger sense of self when they know who their family members are, and what happened in their families in the past;

5. patterns of constructive behavior replace the broken family bonds, where both spoken and unspoken hostilities prevented open communication;

6. special mission grandparents carry the ball responsibly, so that family relationships continue to thrive rather than deteriorate through lack of attention;

7. families become more meaningful arenas, and more in touch with community needs, because they are less focused on merely trying to survive as independent units.

As special mission grandparents come full circle in restoring balance to their fragmented families, they express themselves to their grandchildren through their different kinds of community involvement. This kind of giving to others is an inspiration, and even when families have been badly fragmented and need much work and attention before they are whole and balanced, community contributions also need to be made.

Hosin continues to busy himself with local Korean cultural events, as well as to persist in his efforts to get reconnected with his family in Korea. His grandchildren accompany him to both the local events and his visits to Korea. Yanfu's progress in learning the Korean language enabled her grandchildren to become increasingly familiar with Korean. Megan undertook more responsibilities in her volunteer counseling position with pregnant teens, and her grandchildren admire her for her dedication to her work. Gilroy's involvement in local politics is a family affair, and his grandchildren benefit from helping behind the scenes at elections and other political gatherings.

Thus fragmented families can be brought into balance not only within themselves, but also with respect to their intrinsic connectedness to communities. Family members need to meet their own emotional needs and then examine how they can contribute to wider social arenas. Increasing cooperative action is a goal for families and also for communities and society. Special mission grandparents can only ensure a better future for their grandchildren when this principle is applied to solving social problems.

12

Blended Families

Blended families are made up of more than the usual number of different families due to shifts in their relationships that followed divorces, remarriages, and deaths. Blended families are also called *reconstituted families*, because their different kinds of structures reflect the ways in which a larger kin group has been put together following these particular kinds of upheavals. Historically the prevalence of divorce and remarriage in modern society has led to the emergence of more blended families than ever before.

Special mission grandparents play an important role in blended families. Although blended families gain many varied advantages from special mission grandparents, they benefit particularly from both their emotional support and their direct interventions on behalf of their grandchildren. These grandparents purposely keep all their family relationships as open and as connected to each other as possible, thereby decreasing the likelihood that the remarried stepfamilies will develop rigid traditional patterns, intense conflicts, severe dysfunctions, problematic emotional distance, or irreparable schisms.

When grandparents cultivate meaningful contacts with a large number of their family members, they strengthen their strategic generational positions, and they increase their capacities to make effective interventions for the purpose of building strong relationships. In the long run grandparents' full participation in their wider kin groups enables them to balance their blended families and to create a whole from the different additions and subtractions to their original families.

Special mission grandparents also make a habit of focusing more on their own grandchildren than on their stepgrandchildren, so that they do not encroach on the cares and concerns of other grandparents or other families. This strategy reduces the complexity of many blended families, where multiple marriages have made relating to a large number of grandchildren and stepgrandchildren difficult or even unmanageable.

Special mission grandparents make sure that they have good working relationships with their own adult children in their blended families. They make this a priority, rather than aim to please their in-laws. They do this because they know that the original bonds of parent and adult child are rock-bottom foundations for the new complex blended families and because their access to their grandchildren is controlled by their adult children.

Carmen, Soto, Yvonne, and Jamison have been concerned about the ungainly growth of their blended families for many years. Although Carmen and Soto have lived together for almost thirty years, their three adult children have each had multiple partners and several children. One of their daughters has three children who have different fathers, and a son has been married and divorced twice. Yvonne and Jamison have been married for about ten years, and they have each been married before. Yvonne has two children from her first marriage and one from her second marriage. Although Yvonne did not have any children with Jamison, Jamison has two children from a prior marriage, and one child from a relationship he had before he married Yvonne.

Although multiple marriages alone produce a large kin group, relationship complexities increase when children from in-law connections are added to the mix. Carmen and Soto had seven stepgrandchildren as well as eight grandchildren. Their stepgrandchildren belong to the spouses or partners of their adult children. Similarly, Yvonne and Jamison have eight stepgrandchildren as well as their eight grandchildren, and even though some of these stepgrandchildren disappeared when marriages and relationships broke up, some contacts have been maintained.

In order to manage these large numbers of grandchildren and stepgrandchildren, Carmen and Soto decided to follow the lead of their children. Where their adult children remained close to their stepchildren, Carmen and Soto have similarly tried to maintain contact with them, and they include these particular stepgrandchildren in their activities with their own grandchildren. Even this simplification is emotionally difficult and costly, however, especially when it comes to paying for travel or throwing birthday parties.

Yvonne and Jamison decided on a different strategy to manage their relationships with their large brood of grandchildren and stepgrandchildren. They did what was most convenient for them, thereby essentially ignoring their grandchildren and stepgrandchildren who lived far away or whose parents could not bring them to visit. By doing this they cut down on the number of their grandparenting relationships pretty drastically, as several of their grandchildren and stepgrandchildren lived in fairly distant places and did not visit Yvonne and Jamison often.

Listening to some of the comments of Carmen, Soto, Yvonne, and Jamison provides a measure of their frustration and dissatisfaction with continuing to grandparent in these ways. Carmen, Soto, Yvonne, and Jamison all wanted to improve their relationships with their grandchildren and to avoid the penalties of being members of blended families.

"Grandparenting today is not like it was when I was a child," says Carmen. "My grandparents had a lot of grand-

children, but they knew whether they were coming or going. There was a certain stability in their lives that we seem
to have lost. Somehow I can wake up to find that I have
one more stepgrandchild, or that my daughter-in-law has
moved away with my grandchild."

"I am not sure that we have a final count of our grandchildren and stepgrandchildren," says Soto. "It is really
difficult for me to make a difference in my grandchildren's
lives when I am not sure of who they are or where they are.
I don't suppose we are alone in this, but grandparenting
should be so much more than sending birthday cards."

"I know I am part of my own grandparenting muddle,
but I never thought about grandparenting when I went
through two marriages and then met Jamison" philo-
sophiced Yvonne. "I even have stepgrandchildren from
my first two marriages who I see from time to time. It
makes me wonder as to what a grandparent is supposed to
do, or how I can be a real grandparent to at least some of
my grandchildren."

"My own instability in relationships is matched only by
that of my children!" exclaims Jamison. "I knew when I
was younger that I was not setting a good example for my
children, but I never felt as though I could do better. I am
concerned that I am going to spend the rest of my life picking
up pieces and trying to make sense of all this confusion."

Carmen, Soto, Yvonne, and Jamison became interested in
following guidelines to improve the quality of their grandparenting in their blended families because they were desperate to
find ways to increase the number of meaningful relationships
they had with their grandchildren. At the same time, they were
overwhelmed by their sheer numbers. It was because Carmen,
Soto, Yvonne, and Jamison felt responsible for so many of their
grandchildren and stepgrandchildren that nothing seemed rewarding, and their guilt and anxiety were easily provoked.

Developing a special mission as grandparents begins in part with cutting down grandparenting tasks to reasonable proportions. When Carmen, Soto, Yvonne, and Jamison concentrated their grandparenting only on their adult children's children, their grandparenting responsibilities were much simplified. Rather than follow along with their adult children's patterns of parenting, as Carmen and Soto had done, and rather than see only those grandchildren and stepgrandchildren who lived close by, as Yvonne and Jamison had done, they began to sort out which of their grandchildren were most important to them.

Special mission grandparenting is also based on the principle that grandchildren should be treated pretty equally, wherever they happen to live. Plans have to be made, so that grandparents can organize ways to connect with their distant grandchildren as well as those who live in their home state. In fact, it is only in this way that grandparents can keep all their key relationships as open and as meaningful as possible.

When Carmen, Soto, Yvonne, and Jamison began to focus on their adult children's children, they felt relieved of the inordinate burden of having to respond to both their grandchildren and their stepgrandchildren. They were able to discover more about their grandchildren's interests and to include them in family events, some of which have involved travel. It was easier for them to find more opportunities to build one-on-one relationships with their grandchildren, and they also had sufficient emotional resources left to develop their own outside interests and community activities.

One of the things that Carmen, Soto, Yvonne, and Jamison noticed when they made these changes in relating to their grandchildren was that their bonds with their adult children also improved. Rather than spreading themselves too thin by trying to cater to the needs of their stepgrandchildren as well as their grandchildren, they were able to improve the quality of their grandparenting. Even though making this move meant that inevitably some stepgrandchildren had fewer privileges because their own grandparents did not keep in touch with them, in most cases parents or other family members were available to meet the needs of the stepgrandchildren.

Like special mission grandparents in other kinds of families, Carmen, Soto, Yvonne, and Jamison had difficulty in getting started to bring balance to their blended families. They had long been overwhelmed by the complexities of the relationships among their relatives, in-laws, and steprelatives, and it was not immediately clear to them what their priorities should be. They only knew that they wanted to improve their grandparenting, as well as to simplify their relationships with their grandchildren and stepgrandchildren. They were aware of having interests beyond their families that they had never had the time or energy to honor, and they were intrigued by the idea of actually aiming to become involved in meaningful community ventures.

In order for Carmen, Soto, Yvonne, and Jamison to make more sense out of their individual grandparenting situations in their blended families, it is useful to look more closely at what it means to be a member of a blended family. Some of the following characteristics apply to their blended families and to the blended families of other special mission grandparents:

1. blended families can be more precarious than other families, in that the higher incidences of divorce and separation in blended families can create more overnight additions and subtractions of family members than usually happens in other families;

2. because of their large number of in-laws and steprelatives, blended families may be more extensive, and therefore involve their members in more complex relationships, than other kinds of families;

3. the larger kin group of blended families can make their members feel more secure and more integrated into

the world at large, as it seems to provide more personal security than an isolated nuclear family, which is made up only of parents and children;

4. blended families frequently have more breathing space for their members as they can come and go freely, and are not often subjected to close supervision;

5. blended families may be more realistic in their expectations for each other because their members have frequently weathered more pain and despair than members of other kinds of families;

6. blended families may have some social stigma in communities where more conventional or traditional values prevail;

7. blended families may be less connected to past generations than other families, because they have broken away from their elders, and have not allowed past values to influence their actions;

8. blended families may be more inclined to launch their members into society than other families, because their social worth is less caught up in family customs per se.

Given these distinctive characteristics of blended families, Carmen, Soto, Yvonne, and Jamison proceeded to try to bring balance to their blended families. Their particular initiatives as special mission grandparents reflect what they think about themselves, their families, their grandchildren, and their communities.

SPECIAL MISSION GRANDPARENTS AND BLENDED FAMILIES

When Carmen decided to relate more closely to her grandchildren than to her stepgrandchildren, she had to deal with some criticism from her adult children, as well as some disappointment from some of her stepgrandchildren.

Soto had a similar experience when he too cut back on his grandparenting and concentrated only on his own grandchildren. He started to take his grandchildren with him to more sports events, and he went for walks with them. He was happy not to follow his adult children's leads in how to grandparent, and he drew his grandchildren into his volunteer work at his local church.

Yvonne started to make contact with more family members when she went further afield to visit her grandchildren. Her regular visits to her grandchildren built a relationship network that added stability to their blended family. As she brought her blended family more into balance, she was able to take up aerobics at a local health club, and she included her grandchildren in a variety of athletic pursuits.

Jamison began to travel more in order to build relationships with his geographically distant grandchildren. He made contact with many relatives he had lost touch with over the years, and by reviving these bonds he stabilized his blended family and helped to bring it into balance. Jamison's relationships with his distant adult children improved, and he felt that his life was more meaningful than it had been in recent years.

Special mission grandparents in blended families have a responsibility to try to reactivate the basic structures of their families, so that their grandchildren can have greater emotional security and a stronger sense of belonging. When the original families stay connected within the blended families, they provide a foundation or firm basis for in-law and stepfamily relationships, which are often superimposed on the original families.

Carmen, Soto, Yvonne, and Jamison managed to strengthen their family bonds with their adult children, and as a result, the flow of grandparenting in their blended families was uninterrupted. By staying in touch with their own brothers and sisters, their adult children, and their grandchildren, the original kin group became more cohesive. Although Carmen, Soto, Yvonne, and Jamison continued to be respectful to their in-laws and stepfamilies, they did not express their energies in these relationships as much as they had done in the past. By releasing some of the energy they had invested in grandparenting their stepgrandchildren, they were able to enrich their relationships with their grandchildren.

BLENDED FAMILIES AND CHANGE

Bringing blended families into balance means that these families are strengthened. Because the basic bonds of blended families are now better maintained, their relationships become more firm or more clearly defined, as well as more flexible. Family members gain from the increased security of the newly balanced blended families, and at the same time they are freer to go out into the world to do what they really want to do. Therefore, when blended families are balanced they not only strengthen their immediate communities, but they also allow their family members to make contributions to change that extend outside their own communities.

Balancing blended families makes them free of many of the negative consequences of divorce and death. In other words, balanced blended families give sufficient security to their family members—particularly to their grandchildren—so that they do not suffer from the most drastic relationship shocks associated with divorces and deaths. Because the extended kin of balanced blended families are so active, they are more able to meet the emotional needs of their relatives.

Special mission grandparents expedite the ways in which blended families participate in broad change processes. Carmen began to teach history to senior citizens, and she engaged her grandchildren in helping her to enroll participants in her classes.

Some of her grandchildren also attended her lectures, and they learned a great deal from listening to Carmen's presentations.

Soto started to work with a Boy Scout troop at his church after he had done as much as he could to bring his blended family into balance and improve his grandparenting. His activities with his grandchildren included visits to sports events, walks, and camping trips with a Scout troop which has many underprivileged boys.

Yvonne became certified as an aerobics instructor, and she took a part-time job at a local health club. She was given a free pass for her grandchildren to use the children's equipment at the club, and they gained self confidence from this opportunity to exercise and from the time they spend with their grandmother at the health club.

Jamison started to write a family history and enjoyed reading it to his grandchildren. He involved his grandchildren in his research on the family, which included using library records. Jamison served on the board of his local public library, and through contacts he made with public schools in the area, they formed a coalition to improve their library resources.

Therefore, Carmen, Soto, Yvonne, and Jamison all contributed to community changes outside their families as part of their special mission as grandparents. They did what they enjoyed doing, involved their grandchildren in their community activities, and worked hard to achieve their goals. Because Carmen, Soto, Yvonne, and Jamison were effective in their communities as well as in their families, their grandchildren saw them as agents of change and were interested in following their examples.

Even though blended families are made up of many different families, they work together more or less coherently as a whole, especially if their basic structures are strong. Special mission grandparents who are members of blended families are instrumental in activating that basic structure and in keeping it moving along. When grandparents pay closer attention to their own adult children and their offspring, the probabilities for destructive conflict and estrangement in their blended families are reduced. Furthermore, their grandchildren benefit from having more tenacious emotional connections and an enhanced sense of security.

When blended families have flexible, open relationships, they may be richer sources of security and inspiration than other kinds of families. Because blended families have more complex relationships, their increased number of kin may enrich family life in untold ways. However, because blended families are frequently precarious, in that their relationships are not as grounded in generational continuities, they may also be unstable and unable to give their members a sufficient sense of belonging.

Some of the ways in which special mission grandparents bring balance to their blended families and some of the ways in which they make contributions through their blended families are:

1. they define family lines through their adult children and members of past generations so that each family within a blended family retains its own characteristics;
2. they give priority to their grandchildren through their adult children, rather than to their stepgrandchildren;
3. they keep family relationships as open and as interesting as possible, in order to increase the flexibility of their family bonds;
4. they do what they can to improve their grandparenting, and then concentrate on finding ways to attend to community tasks;
5. they include their grandchildren as much as possible in their community endeavors, and teach them that being

a member of a family includes having a responsibility to improve the lot of those who are less fortunate;

6. they write family histories, take photographs, send E-mail, make trips, organize family reunions, and attend major family events in order to maintain contact with as many family members as possible;

7. they do their part in decreasing estrangements that have developed due to family deaths and divorces, and they mediate where feuding family members refuse to enter into direct communication with each other.

Carmen, Soto, Yvonne, and Jamison did some of these things to ensure that their grandchildren would not suffer from the negative consequences of being members of blended families. Their successes in developing their community interests are a measure of the impact they had on their families, and their grandchildren benefitted both directly and indirectly from the moves they made in their kin groups and in their communities.

Thus special mission grandparents have a constructive role to play in making sure that blended families become as strong and as healthy as possible. Even though blended families may benefit most from having the cooperation of several family members to achieve these goals, it still takes only one special mission grandparent to make a change in existing patterns of family behavior for there to be ripples of effects in that family and its community.

III

ACCOMPLISHING THE SPECIAL MISSION

13

From Generation to Generation

Accomplishing the special mission of grandparents means living fully for self and, at the same time, moving towards the most meaningful and most constructive family and community well-being possible. Passing on hard-earned wisdom to grandchildren is satisfying, because there is a real possibility that grandparents can make a major difference in their grandchildren's lives. Therefore, as grandchildren set out in life, grandparents' contributions reach into the indefinite future.

In order to understand family interaction and grandparenting opportunities, we must go beyond conventional and commercial definitions of grandparenting. Special agent grandparents are authentic and true to themselves in all their actions, which enables them to make their greatest and most significant contributions. Grandparents accomplish their special mission when they develop their own distinctive styles of grandparenting and create conditions that improve the overall well-being of their families and communities. Because grandparents have an advantageous generational position in their families, they can help many family relationships become more viable. In fact, it is this same outward-looking posture to life that also enables them to make broad social contributions.

Only at death is the special mission of grandparents accomplished, although some special agent grandparents have a continuing influence on others after they are deceased. The legacies of special agent grandparents can become a living heritage for future generations, families, and society.

However, in many respects our contributions as grandparents are signed and sealed when we die whether we like it or not and whether we accepted the special mission of grandparents or not. But life goes on after we die, not only within the small nuclear families of parents and children, but also within the vast connectedness between different generations. Whoever we are, whatever our circumstances, and whether we are dead or alive, we are part of a sea of generational relationships that flows from the dim past to an unforeseen future.

If we grandparent more or less unconsciously or automatically, without taking the special mission of grandparents seriously, we merely react to family pressures rather than create more life-enhancing patterns of interdependence. When we do not modify our existing family relationships, we are essentially trapped in a status quo of repeated behavior between generations. Furthermore, the push and pull from our intergenerational enmeshment makes us passive and inhibits our abilities to act freely and constructively within our families and in society.

By contrast, when we accept and follow the special mission of grandparents to the best of our abilities, we not only live more fully, but also shield our grandchildren and their progeny from the most negative consequences of family problems. Our actions free our adult children from negative family intensities, as well as our grandchildren, thereby enabling them to move more freely into communities and society.

Glen, Annette, Albert, and Lois are grandparents in fairly well-balanced families, who live in the suburbs of the same small town. Their families moved to this area several generations ago. Glen and Annette are unaware of their family histories and the ways in which the different generations of their families have continued particular behavior patterns through the generations. They think that they are very different from their own parents and grandparents and that they do not have much of an impact on their grandchildren. By contrast, Albert and Lois are both familiar with their family histories. Albert has been interested in putting the picture of his family together since he was a small boy, and Lois had a favorite aunt who was her family's historian and who taught her much until her death. Albert and Lois are more interested in grandparenting than Glen and Annette. They are aware of some of the continuities through the generations, and they believe that they can have a strong impact on the lives of their grandchildren.

"I don't know much about my family history," says Glen. "I don't think that matters very much, because I can't influence my children or grandchildren anyway."

"The past is important, I know," says Annette, "but only those events that affect everyone in society. I don't see how knowing anything about the past generations of my family affects anyone at all."

"I am very glad that I spent so much time getting to know my family's history," says Albert. "I believe that what I can tell my grandchildren about their great-grandparents, great-uncles, and great-aunts influences important choices they have to make. In fact, telling them about their family's history may be one of the most powerful ways that I can be a grandfather."

"I loved my aunt so much from when I was a very young child, and I grew up learning about our family history from her," says Lois. "I have been able to make use of this vital information in my own life, and I am quite dedicated to teaching my grandchildren about what went on in our family in the past. Even when my grandchildren don't want to listen to me, I find ways to communicate the gist of what needs to be said, and somehow it gets heard. These are important life lessons."

Special mission grandparents respect intergenerational con-tinuities in their families. They may not know all the details of their family histories, but they take every opportunity to collect information about their past relatives and their elders as a way to immunize themselves from needlessly repeating the worst be-havior characteristics of their families. That is to say that these grandparents have a sense of the power of intergenerational rootedness in their families, as well as a sense of their own im-portance as grandparents in these chains of behavior.

Special mission grandparents also know that in order to take charge of their lives and those of their grandchildren, they need to be able to interrupt the cycles of destructive behavior that get transmitted between generations. That is, if there is a pattern of accidental deaths in the past generations of a family, it is easier not to repeat these circumstances in present generations if fam-ily members have a knowledge about these unfortunate events and specific ways to avoid getting into similar situations. In sum, heightening awareness of this intergenerational pattern can save grandchildren's lives, whereas ignoring this kind of his-tory will increase the likelihood that accidental deaths will re-peat in the generations to come.

Glen and Annette have some negative behavior patterns in their past generations. Glen's family has a history of alcoholism among its male family members, and Annette's family has sev-eral women members who had children at very young ages, sometimes out of wedlock, who struggled with burdens of re-sponsibility and insufficient financial means. The alcoholism in Glen's family had a negative impact on many family mem-bers, and Glen considered himself to be an alcoholic. Also, in Annette's family the women who had children at very young ages, or out of wedlock, did not do well in life because they were poor, had little education, and bore more children than was healthy for them. Several of these women died prematurely and without family support.

Albert and Lois knew some details about the most important problems in their families' past. Albert's family had a large number of health problems associated with heart disease, for men and women alike, while Lois's family showed patterns of teenagers who dropped out of school and did not complete their education. Because Albert and Lois knew some of these circumstances, they made sure that their children and grand-children were told about their different family weaknesses. Knowing that they may be inclined to repeat unhealthy eating and exercise habits, or that they may resist staying in school to further their education, helped Albert's and Lois's children and grandchildren to be cautious about letting their feelings take over their lives. If they acted thoughtlessly, they could fall into a groove where these problem behaviors appeared to be attractive alternatives. On the other hand, if they made a habit of carefully considering what the consequences of their actions would be, they could prevent the negative consequences of heart disease and dropping out of school.

In these ways Albert, Lois, and their grandchildren were able to be in control of their lives more than Glen, Annette, and their grandchildren. Knowing the past put Albert and Lois at an ad-vantage for not repeating the past, and this know-how gave them a sense of being able to influence the lives of their grand-children in very significant ways. If Albert and Lois can prevent premature death or lack of education for their grandchildren, they have essentially transformed some of the givens of their life chances.

Therefore, special mission grandparents not only try to dis-cover more about their family histories, but they also design family interventions to interrupt the hold of negative behavior patterns on current generations. It is not enough for grandpar-ents to spend quality time with their grandchildren, or to in-volve them in their communities, but they also need to educate their grandchildren so that they want to continue the most posi-tive things possible about their family heritages. Special mission grandparents teach their grandchildren to see, hear, and tell, so that they will be more knowledgeable and wiser about what is passed on in their families from generation to generation.

Special mission grandparents find out as much as they can about their own particular placement between the generations of their families. They put themselves in the context of the intergenerational flow of behavior and assess to what extent they are successful at carrying on the most constructive aspects of the behavior of their own grandparents and other relatives who lived in the past.

If this kind of specific research is not possible, grandparents can purposely develop a sense of continuities in their families and see how chains of behavior restrict or free their family members, particularly their grandchildren. Intergenerational links set the scene for defining ways in which special mission grandparents can make their most significant moves in the present.

Because of their lack of knowledge about their families' past behavior, Glen and Annette were further away from being special mission grandparents than Albert and Lois. Also, because Glen and Annette did not even value the process of compiling a family history, let alone pay attention to family history, their grandchildren are more likely to suffer from negative behavior patterns that have been passed down through the generations than the grandchildren of Albert and Lois. Being a special mission grandparent is therefore a great deal about having a certain kind of historical awareness and an inclination to make connections between events of the past and current situations.

Special mission grandparents pay attention to the following aspects of intergenerational behavior:

1. repetitions in the behavior of family members in different generations;

2. assessments of the destructiveness of these patterns of behavior, especially for their grandchildren;

3. opportunities to interrupt sequences of behavior that have a negative impact on family members;

4. resistance to change, especially when behavior has been truly ingrained for several generations;

5. key players in perpetuating behavior that has been repeated through the generations;

6. ways to undo their own participation in intergenerational transmissions;

7. ways to shield their grandchildren from the impact of ever-increasing negative consequences from problematic intergenerational exchanges;

8. possibilities for encouraging relatives to combine forces to bring about new patterns of behavior in current generations.

Glen and Annette were not open to the idea that past generations can influence current behavior negatively, so they did not think it important to shield their grandchildren from any negative consequences from past generations. Albert and Lois wanted to get to know more about the past generations in their families so that they could do a better job of being prepared to teach their grandchildren to avoid these pitfalls.

Thus special mission grandparents not only have to be torchbearers in making efforts to stop the chain reaction of behavior repetitions between generations, but they also need to teach their grandchildren how to protect themselves from dragons of the past that lurk in the present. It is only when their grandchildren understand some of these dangers that they will be able to truly fend for themselves and ward off any inclinations they have to get bogged down in these currents of negative intergenerational connections.

SPECIAL MISSION GRANDPARENTS AND GENERATIONS

Because grandparents are usually the oldest survivors in their families, it may be difficult for them to compile family histories from the oral reports of members of any other generation but their own. However, one of the primary goals of special mission grandparents is to cultivate a questioning awareness about the past, so that at each opportunity they try to discover more of what went on in prior generations. This kind of openness is a powerful step towards breaking cycles of negative behavior that have been transmitted through past and current generations.

As long as Glen and Annette cannot be dissuaded from their view that whatever members of the past generations of their families have done, these actions are unimportant and insignificant for present family members, it is unlikely that they will become special mission grandparents. Special mission grandparents deliberately develop a historical perspective from knowledge about their families' past generations, in order to be effective in their families and communities, and in order to influence their grandchildren's development. Although having a historical awareness is not in and of itself a guarantee that grandparents will be able to carry through with a special mission to improve their grandparenting, it is necessary to know something about the kinds of exchanges that took place between members of past generations, in order to develop a realistic perspective on grandparenting.

By contrast, both Albert and Lois are able to grasp the importance of intergenerational connectedness and to focus sufficiently on the past in order to become special mission grandparents. Seeing patterns of alcoholism and disastrously early motherhood in their families helped them to discuss these issues with their grandchildren, including the fact that their grandchildren might easily react to alcohol and sex in inappropriate ways because of this past.

Ideally, special mission grandparents assess their own tasks in their families and in their communities with close regard for what has gone on in their families in past generations. They see that without a conscious, deliberate effort on their parts, unwanted and unproductive behavior may be automatically passed on to their grandchildren. Special mission grandparents recognize the restrictive power of negative generational transmissions, and they respectfully describe and forewarn their grandchildren about the odds of this happening to them. Special mission grandparents also intervene in ongoing exchanges among family members to open up relationships and to reduce the likelihood of mechanistic repetitions of behavior through the generations.

As a consequence of Glen's and Annette's disinterest in generational transmissions, Glen's family continued to have alcoholic men in the current generations, and the women in Annette's family continued to not do well throughout their lives, especially after they had given birth at very young ages. However, the special mission grandparent efforts of Albert and Lois had more positive results. The heart disease in Albert's family was much reduced, and Lois's family had higher educational achievement in the youngest generation than ever before. Therefore, Albert's and Lois's grandchildren benefitted from their special mission interventions.

GENERATIONS AND CHANGE

Families are slow to change, and when behavior patterns are transmitted between different generations, these are particularly resistant to efforts to shift them. Where no particular interventions are made to interrupt or modify negative behavior that has occurred in past generations, members of present generations find themselves compelled to repeat these same patterns.

Special mission grandparents assume a responsibility to derail the kind of negative behavior that will harm the development of their grandchildren. To save their grandchildren from thought-less and mindless repetitions, special mission grandparents de-vise ways to intervene and channel energy into more constructive patterns. Only through knowing something about the relentlessness of these patterns can grandparents be suffi-ciently motivated to make these kinds of changes.

Glen and Annette operated in a no-change situation because they were unwilling to connect the past, the present, and the fu-ture in terms of the unique patterns of behavior in their families. Glen's and Annette's reluctance to make changes meant that the status quo of their families was preserved for one more gen-eration at least and that their grandchildren were not shielded from the patterns of alcoholism and young motherhood in their respective families.

In contrast, Albert's and Lois's commitments to make as many changes as possible in their families motivated them to in-terrupt negative behavior in their families. They made it known that they were unwilling to participate in imbalances in family exchanges, rigidities in views and actions, secret-keeping, and actions that limited family members' freedom and autonomy. Their planned and spontaneous interventions helped to turn the tide in the behavior patterns in these families sufficiently so that family members were less symptomatic in their physical health and more successful in their education. Albert's and Lois's grandchildren benefitted a great deal from their initia-tives, and their development was much less problematic than would have been the case if Albert and Lois had not taken their special mission as grandparents seriously.

In addition to these family changes, Albert and Lois were able to participate more fully in their communities. Albert helped to organize a free clinic for health care in a poor neigh-borhood, and Lois volunteered as a career counselor in that same poor neighborhood. Their grandchildren benefitted from seeing their committed grandparents work in their community, and Albert's and Lois's compassion for others encouraged them to consider how they might make their own kinds of contributions to those who are less fortunate than themselves.

Glen and Annette continued to be so caught up in their family problems that, unlike Albert and Lois, they had no time and energy to spend in activities outside their families. Glen had even more problems with alcohol, and Annette became seriously ill with a chronic blood disease she had suffered from for many years. Thus Glen and Annette became victims of their own intergenerational patterns, rather than grandparents with a special mission to change this ongoing behavior.

Grandparents can expect some of the following results if they pay attention to patterns of negative behavior that have been repeated from generation to generation, and if they act sufficiently effectively to change these patterns:

1. their families will be characterized by increased balance, with relationships that are free and autonomous;

2. rigid behavior patterns in the past generations of a family will no longer be repeated, or will be sufficiently modified so that they will not compel the youngest family members to be drawn into them;

3. family members will do better in life, and grandchildren will develop as strong individuals;

4. grandchildren will learn to respect the power of the past, so that they help to maintain the conditions necessary to prevent negative patterns from reappearing;

5. special mission grandparents will continue to educate other family members about the importance of keeping relationships open and balanced, in order to prevent intergenerational problems;

6. achieving successful changes in negative behavior patterns is no guarantee that these new patterns will con-

tinue, because there must be an ongoing effort to prevent problematic behavior from developing;

7. special mission grandparents who manage to neutralize generational impediments can make more meaningful commitments to get involved in their communities;

8. grandchildren will learn from the example of their special mission grandparents how to give to their communities as well as to their families.

Although Glen and Annette could not share these benefits of becoming special mission grandparents with their families, Albert and Lois were able to initiate significant changes in their family relationships. In spite of the fact that negative behavior patterns are not the only influences that are passed on from generation to generation, it is the negative patterns of behavior that have the most power to interrupt the healthy development of grandchildren. These influences are so strong that they outweigh the advantages that can be passed on to grandchildren from past generations.

14

Leaving a Legacy

The most precious legacy special mission grandparents can leave their grandchildren is to tell them how to live well and generously, and according to their own most cherished values. When grandparents cultivate meaning in their own lives, they become real-life examples for their grandchildren to follow, and when grandparents are consistent in putting their most cherished values into action, they increase the likelihood that their grandchildren will follow suit. Inheriting material possessions, although always significant, is not as useful to grandchildren in the long run as gaining the kind of wisdom and skills that will carry them and their families forward for a lifetime.

The legacies special mission grandparents leave their grandchildren provide links to the wider society as well as to their family histories. The beliefs and actions of special mission grandparents maintain an outward-looking family culture, which encourages their families to launch members into communities and society to make substantial unique contributions.

Even though all grandparents necessarily forge some kind of relationship with society, these bonds are often relatively impersonal and anonymous. This is why it is primarily through family exchanges that the most personal and most meaningful legacies of special mission grandparents are formed. Thus the substance of grandparents' lives becomes the most precious of gems to be passed on to their grandchildren and other relatives.

Dawn, Gary, Georgia, and Ron are grandparents of middle-class means who have each been college educated. Dawn and Gary worked in their own small retail business for thirty years, and they are well known in their small town. They have three children and five grandchildren who live close by. Georgia and Ron were health professionals in a state agency for many years, until they retired in order to travel and pursue a variety of hobbies. Even though they have lived in the same small town for more than twenty years, they do not know their neighbors well. They have two children and four grandchildren who live in the same state.

Dawn and Gary wanted to leave their grandchildren a legacy that would help them to remember Dawn and Gary, as well as help them to do well in difficult times. Dawn and Gary had been successful in their marriage and in their business because they know how to relate to other people, and they want to communicate these skills to their young grandchildren.

Georgia and Ron were very relieved to get out of the rat race of their competitive work situations when they retired. They decided that what they want to do most of all is to travel and that somehow they would try to keep in touch with their friends and relatives. Georgia and Ron are hazy about having any particular goals to achieve with their grandchildren, and they think that because they do not intend to spend all their financial resources traveling and pursuing other leisure activities, their remaining assets will be their legacy for them.

"I love my grandchildren dearly," says Dawn, "and I would give anything to be able to help them to be successful. I've had many struggles myself, but I have become strong and I know how to cope, and how to get things done. I want to pass on my know-how to my grandchildren, so that they won't have to be unproductive in their lives."

"I never imagined that being a grandparent would be so important to me," says Gary. "I want to leave my grandchildren some wisdom about making the most of who they are, but it's not easy to know how to do this. I hope my grandchildren will develop into strong and compassionate individuals."

"I am looking forward to retirement very much," says Georgia. "It's good to have raised our children, and now it is our children's turn to raise their children. I can't wait to get out in the world, and really be footloose and fancy-free."

"Australia, here we come!" exclaims Ron. "I have longed for this kind of freedom for many years, and I can't wait to make the break. No one will miss us—this is really a golden age! I know things will be well taken care of in our family when we are not around."

It was largely due to their different visions of their roles as grandparents, and to their different degrees of commitment and interest in leaving legacies for their grandchildren, that Dawn, Gary, Georgia, and Ron pursued contrasting paths as grandparents. Because Dawn and Gary are galvanized by their desires to leave a particular kind of legacy for their grandchildren, they make the most of relating to their grandchildren in their own chosen ways now. On the other hand, Georgia and Ron have essentially relinquished what might be thought of as their grandparenting responsibilities to their adult children.

Because of these articulated differences in their ideas about leaving their grandchildren a legacy, it was only Dawn and Gary who made deliberate efforts to include their grandchildren in their different activities. As Dawn's and Gary's travel had customarily revolved around visiting their geographically distant relatives, and because they are interested in family history, they decided to make contact with relatives they have never met and relatives they see only rarely. Because Dawn and Gary have spent much time with their grandchildren since they were born, they try to take their grandchildren with them on these travels whenever they can. They take just a single grandchild along with them when this is easier for them to manage, and it turns out that the chosen grandchild usually finds it particularly enjoyable to have their undivided attention.

By contrast, Georgia and Ron organize their travel around tourist spots and packaged tours to exotic places. They are motivated primarily by an urge to get away from it all, and a desire to see the world, rather than any wish to explore relationships that had influenced, and still influence, the quality of their emotional well-being. Georgia and Ron expressly do not want to take their grandchildren with them when they travel, and they strongly prefer to drop in to visit their grandchildren when it is convenient for them to do so between trips. Georgia and Ron keep up with sending birthday and holiday gifts to their grandchildren, but they are not particularly concerned about how their grandchildren are being brought up, or how they can contribute to their welfare.

Thus Dawn and Gary essentially adopted a special mission as grandparents, in that they resolved to give their grandchildren a firm foundation of knowledge to help them to be effective in the world. However, Georgia and Ron are so preoccupied with organizing travel and leisure pursuits for their own enjoyment that they fall into a rut of being rather conventional and commercial in expressing themselves as grandparents. Because Dawn and Gary were conscious of the kind of legacy they wanted to leave their grandchildren, they conducted their lives in ways that related directly to their ideas of what this legacy should be. On the other hand, Georgia and Ron considered that their legacy to their grandchildren would be the remainder of what they owned after they had traveled and entertained themselves through leisure activities. Georgia and Ron planned to spend whatever they needed to spend for their travel and hobbies, and their residual financial resources would then become their legacy for their grandchildren.

Like Dawn and Gary, special mission grandparents give much thought as to what their legacies for their grandchildren will be. One of the ways in which these grandparents want their lives to have meaning is through how they think their grandchildren will remember them when they are dead. They know that they can influence their grandchildren to some extent from the grave, and they want to make the most of this privilege by finding the most effective and most constructive ways to have an impact on them. Putting a legacy together to leave to their grandchildren also links their experiences of the past, present, and future, and this helps special mission grandparents to cultivate and retain a broad perspective in choosing how to spend their time and energy.

Considering what legacy to leave grandchildren is a serious business, and these ideas influence grandparents' behavior. Special mission grandparents understand the importance of leaving financial resources to grandchildren, but they also want to have more of an impact on the emotional quality of their grandchildren's lives. Some of their considerations about leaving a legacy to their grandchildren include:

1. understanding the ways in which their grandchildren need assistance to face life squarely and to make the most of their opportunities;

2. finding out how to communicate effectively the wisdom and know-how learned by grandparents, so that grandchildren will not have to repeat their grandparents' mistakes;

3. bringing past, present, and future experiences together, so that grandchildren can benefit from seeing the broader picture of their lives;

4. continuing to make family and community contributions, so that grandparents will be remembered as being an inspiration for their grandchildren;

5. persisting in moves to keep family and community relationships open, so that these initiatives will be continued as part of a living legacy after their deaths;

6. using the idea of leaving a legacy for grandchildren to
   keep checking out what grandparents' priorities and
   preferred goals are;

7. working closely and amicably with adult children so
   that grandparents can continue to have access to the
   day-to-day lives of grandchildren;

8. being in charge of their own physical and emotional
   health, so that their legacies are known and understood
   by their grandchildren before they die.

Dawn and Gary were able to carry through many of these aspects of preparing a legacy for their grandchildren. Although
Georgia and Ron did not give their legacies much thought, they
continued to be examples to their grandchildren of how to live
life fully and to enjoy themselves. They did not leave their
grandchildren a negative legacy—that is, a series of difficult
problems that would be automatically inherited by their grandchildren—but the remainder of their finances was not as valuable a legacy as it could have been.

SPECIAL MISSION GRANDPARENTS AND LEGACIES

Dawn and Gary deliberately draw their grandchildren into
their lives because they want them to feel that they belong to
their family and to know that they are connected to the past.
Dawn and Gary want their grandchildren to develop strong
emotional roots in their family, so that they will be able to go

out into the world and give of themselves to others. Thus the legacy that Dawn and Gary have chosen to leave behind them is their family itself, so that their grandchildren will not feel isolated or rootless in a difficult world.

By contrast, Georgia and Ron do not have any particular plans about what they want to give as a legacy to their grandchildren. They believe that it is their adult children's responsibility to raise their grandchildren, and they do not intend to fill a particular grandparenting role that will meet their grandchildren's needs. They think that they have met their parental responsibilities because their children are grown with families of their own, and now they want to at least temporarily cut off their family ties and enjoy their freedom in ways they have not been able to before now.

Like Dawn and Gary, special mission grandparents try to place their grandchildren in a stream of intergenerational connectedness. Special mission grandparents know that their families are an emotional resource and foundation for their own independence, and they realize that their grandchildren will cope more effectively with their lives in later years if they can stay meaningfully connected to their kin group. Special mission grandparents aim to build flexible but enduring relationships for their grandchildren, with the hope that their grandchildren will be able to follow their example and sustain these kinds of solid relationships for the next generation.

Although Dawn and Gary, as well as Georgia and Ron, give their grandchildren presents on their birthdays and during the holidays, Dawn and Gary know this is an insufficient basis for building a deep relationship with their grandchildren. On the other hand, Georgia and Ron think that gift giving is the essence of grandparenting, and they send souvenirs to their grandchildren from the many different exotic places they visit in their travels. Although Georgia's and Ron's grandchildren always enjoy receiving these gifts, they do not learn much about themselves or their own background from these exchanges, nor do they realize that they might be being shortchanged by Georgia and Ron.

Dawn's and Gary's grandchildren benefit a great deal from meeting different family members through their grandparents. Even though these visits can be boring for their grandchildren some of the time, they have developed a strong sense of being in the world from getting to know their different relatives, as well as from sharing a kind of identity with them. Dawn's and Gary's grandchildren meet a wide variety of family members and learn something about the older generations in their family as well as their cousins. Dawn and Gary also pass on information about their family history to their grandchildren, who usually enjoy hearing stories about what their grandparents did when they were children. This accounting of the past helps Dawn's and Gary's grandchildren to develop a historical perspective, which will remain with them as part of their grandparents' legacy.

When special mission grandparents die, they are treasured for having helped the younger generations to make a start and get established in life. Even though this acknowledgment may be given to grandparents before they die, special mission grandparents do not pass anything on to their grandchildren that has strings attached. They give because they want their grandchildren to be strong and not because they want their gratitude.

LEGACIES AND CHANGE

It is only long after special mission grandparents die that the impact of their various family and community contributions can be assessed. Together with the more tangible, external aspects of what these grandparents accomplished are several valuable, invisible achievements. For example, special mission grandparents make a significant difference to the quality of life outcomes of their grandchildren, as well as of their children, and these influences include deep aspects of character as well as the acquisition of particular skills. Therefore, overall, the legacies of special mission grandparents are intimately associated with personal and interpersonal change, as well as broad family and community changes.

Being an agent of change is essential to being a special mission grandparent. Dawn and Gary want to make the world a better place for their grandchildren, and they want to teach their grandchildren values that will make them productive members of their communities as well as their families. Even Georgia and Ron hoped that their grandchildren would do well in life, in spite of their not being willing to make a strong commitment to help this actually happen.

Dawn and Gary made many efforts to communicate their business interests and skills to their grandchildren. They told their grandchildren how they had built their own business and what had made it work, and their grandchildren also saw for themselves how Dawn and Gary related to their relatives and peers. One of Dawn's and Gary's important messages for their grandchildren is to show them how important it is to choose their own goals and how being persistent helps to achieve these goals. Dawn's and Gary's volunteer work in a downtown soup kitchen also inspires their grandchildren to have compassion for those who are less fortunate and to try to improve others' disadvantageous situations.

Georgia and Ron show their grandchildren how to enjoy themselves and how to disregard relationships that they think might hold them back. Although this lesson is not constructive in all circumstances, there is merit to taking specific measures in order to act freely and to taking time out for leisure and pleasure. The fact that Georgia and Ron stayed in touch with their grandchildren was a positive contribution that influenced their healthy development. At least Georgia's and Ron's grandchildren knew who their grandparents were and that they cared enough to send gifts from far-off places. However, the ultimate effect of Georgia's and Ron's legacy is directly related to maintaining the status quo of society or to allowing commercial interests to define the terms of their grandparenting. Because neither Georgia nor Ron had long-standing relationships with their own grandparents, however, their grandparenting could be thought of as progress of sorts through the generations of this family.

Special mission grandparents may be much more involved in creating legacies of social change than Dawn, Gary, Georgia, or Ron. For example, some special mission grandparents may influence national policy decisions, the organization of health or education systems in towns and cities, the quality of state child care and care for the elderly, or community services for disadvantaged children and mothers. What is significant about these grandparents is that they take their talents sufficiently seriously that they are able to make substantial contributions to their communities and society as well as to their families. Their grandchildren benefit a great deal from their grandparents' public and social change legacies, including their possibly more direct work in their families. Because the legacies of special mission grandparents are final statements of who these special mission grandparents are, their impact on change can be long-standing.

Dawn, Gary, Georgia, and Ron use a few different ways to build their legacies. Although there are many variations on the theme of what a legacy of a special mission grandparent may be and how legacies may be created, some of the more critical aspects of such legacies include:

1. open family relationships that support grandchildren and other family members;
2. balanced families that are strong enough to prevent or neutralize the onset of a wide variety of family problems;
3. balanced families that provide equal opportunities for both their grandsons and their granddaughters;

4. flexible family relationships that allow grandchildren to come and go without being restricted by relatives' possessiveness or other kinds of emotional immaturity;

5. families that stay connected and do not become fragmented due to geographical separation or emotional estrangement;

6. a shared willingness among family members to maintain the most viable family relationships through time;

7. community contributions that go well beyond meeting immediate or even long-term family needs;

8. encouragement to make the most of whoever one is, whatever a particular situation may be;

9. communication and interpersonal skills that will prepare grandchildren to enter society on their own terms;

10. unique contributions that inspire other family members to become special mission grandparents in their turn, and to work towards leaving valuable legacies of their own.

Dawn, Gary, Georgia, and Ron all left legacies for their grandchildren, as other grandparents inevitably do whether they intend to or not. The choice that confronts us is the extent to which we are willing to become special mission grandparents, which includes working towards building the kind of legacy we really want to leave for our grandchildren, other relatives, and friends. If we leave our grandparenting to chance, we will not make as effective a contribution to our grandchildren as if we work towards deliberately chosen goals that reflect what we want to contribute to them, our families, and our communities.

15

Giving Back to Society

Giving back to society is the latest stage of the creation and development of grandparents' special mission. The prior stages of formulating and implementing a special mission are largely concerned with opening up family relationships, bringing families into balance, and making connections between members in the different generations of a family.

However, it is critical that eventually the special mission of grandparents include making thoughtful and effective contributions of grandparents' time and energy in social arenas that go well beyond their immediate families. Although strengthening their families undoubtedly has a constructive impact on the well-being of society, when special mission grandparents use their wisdom and emotional security to help to build communities outside their families, they give back to society in ways that make the world go round. Having a stake in what goes on in society further empowers grandparents, increases meaning, and brings recognition from their families and others.

Special mission grandparents' deliberate efforts to give back to society set compelling examples for their grandchildren. The raison d'etre of life and families is not merely to reproduce families, however well-functioning those families may be. Having just this goal is too self-contained to accomplish social progress. Therefore, in order to live up to their responsibilities as citizens, special mission grandparents participate in creative planning, effective decision making, and innovative projects that bring communities together for the purpose of improving social conditions for all.

This human necessity to give back to society in order to live fully calls forth a wide range of grandparents' talents and capacities. Special mission grandparents realize that they must do the best they can to help those who are less privileged than they are and to create conditions that will make the future more satisfying for each member of society. This is an awesome mission, but grandparents are special agents only when they have such broad purposes in mind and move forward to establish their ideals as social realities.

Duane, Theresa, Nigel, and Ginny, who used to be successful professionals, now take their special mission as grandparents very seriously. Duane and Theresa are medical doctors who have been married for thirty-five years. They have three children and five grandchildren. Nigel and Ginny are lawyers who have both had prior marriages. They have been married to each other for fifteen years. They have three children and four grandchildren from their first marriages, as well as two stepgrandchildren, but they do not have any children or grandchildren from their own marriage.

Even though Duane and Theresa were prominent public health officials when they worked, they withdrew from their professional activities when they retired. On the other hand, Nigel and Ginny have become more active in community politics than when they worked as lawyers. Whereas Duane and Theresa want to lead a quieter life now that they have retired, Nigel and Ginny view their retirement as an opportunity to give more of their time and energy to community issues.

"I'm so pleased that my work years are behind me," sighs Duane with a great sense of relief. "I really don't know how I managed to get through those years, and I certainly wouldn't want to repeat them. I look forward to spending the remainder of my years quietly with my family."

"Being a career woman was difficult for me and my children," says Theresa. "I tried hard not to deprive my children of my attention, but I know that this happened sometimes. Perhaps we will be able to make up for it with our grandchildren."

"I'm delighted to be getting more politically involved with my community," says Nigel. "I spent so many years working for clients that it is quite refreshing to address problems directly related to the common good. I'm rather ambitious about trying to make a difference in our youngsters' education."

"How nice it is to have interesting projects that take me out into our community," exclaims Ginny. "For many years I worried myself silly about leaving my children when I went out to work, but now I know that my children and grandchildren are well, and this gives me a great freedom to try to help poor people secure adequate housing. I didn't train as a lawyer for nothing!"

Therefore, although Duane, Theresa, Nigel, and Ginny all take their grandparenting seriously, it is only Nigel and Ginny who enter into community activism seriously. Duane and Theresa have become so private and inward-oriented since their retirement that they have essentially cut themselves off from their external ties and long-standing interests in their community.

Special mission grandparents not only balance their families by opening up their family relationships and establishing equal opportunities for their grandsons and granddaughters to go out into the world, but they also busy themselves with critical community concerns. These grandparents are forward looking, in that they try to find effective ways to accomplish social progress, and they relate to their grandchildren with the ideal of a better future clearly in mind. Special mission grandparents build on their past experiences by becoming involved in solving current problems, so that the future will be better for more people.

Ironically, when grandparents take their grandparenting too seriously, in that they narrow their activities so much that they restrict their comings and goings in the world at large, they cannot give as much to their grandchildren and their families in the long run as if they had stayed involved in their communities. Special mission grandparents find ways to give back to society, so that their grandchildren and relatives will find meaning, purpose, and direction in their everyday activities. Thus grandparents need to see roles for themselves beyond their families if they are to live fully and make their most effective contributions to their families and communities.

Although it is true that some grandparents are so caught up with broad social concerns that they disregard some of their personal responsibilities for their grandchildren, it appears that there are more grandparents who get overinvolved with their families, to the extent that they cannot make adequate contributions to their communities. For example, Nigel and Ginny, like other special mission grandparents, see the broader picture of their lives sufficiently clearly that they interact effectively both in their families and in their communities. In contrast, Duane and Theresa neglect opportunities to participate in their community, so that they can focus more directly on their grandchildren, but by doing this they actually narrow their lives so much that they reduce the impact they can have on their grandchildren's lives.

Special mission grandparents know that they are who they are because of others, and they feel a responsibility to give back to society. They realize that they are privileged to have families, and to be alive, and they want to share their advantages with those who do not have them. They try to improve family and community conditions for the health and well-being of their grandchildren, so that their grandchildren might also acknowledge their good fortune by giving back to society.

Therefore, special mission grandparents give back to society because:

1. this impetus brings them full circle, and their lives gain additional meaning, purpose, and direction from giving back to society;

2. they gain emotional satisfaction from knowing that they are useful in bringing about improved conditions for larger numbers of people;

3. they want their grandchildren to recognize needs outside their family circles;

4. they know they are stronger and more autonomous when they keep their outside interests alive and express them in creative ways;

5. responding to broad social needs allows them to bring past, present, and future concerns together, so that they can act with a deeper sense of integrity;

6. giving to their communities provides a broader and healthier perspective on their situations than being solely focused on their families;

7. gaining recognition in a community brings them some additional status and appreciation from their grandchildren and relatives;

8. being active in community interests is synonymous with living fully, which also gives a strong example to their grandchildren;

9. community projects often include grandchildren's direct participation, which helps them to mature and see the world more realistically;

10. community contributions create a legacy for special mission grandparents, which goes beyond bringing balance to their families.

Thus special mission grandparents are messengers from the real world. They do not succumb to others' definitions of reality, because they are too preoccupied with building their own niches to serve others. They do not translate their family responsibilities narrowly, but rather move out into the world with ever-broadening spheres of influence and contributions.

Although Duane and Theresa are well-educated, successful physicians, they did not extend themselves to public service after their retirement from prestigious paid positions. It is easy to understand why they would consider that their more restful life is well deserved and that they had made many useful contributions to others already, but their lives are not over and they narrow themselves by not using their great potential to continue to give back to society.

The examples of Nigel and Ginny are inspiring to special mission grandparents. Nigel and Ginny are untiring in their efforts to improve educational standards and housing conditions, and they use their expertise for the social good. These are effective ways to give back to society, and their actions benefit their grandchildren, their relatives, and community members as well as themselves.

SPECIAL MISSION GRANDPARENTS AND GIVING BACK TO SOCIETY

Special mission grandparents enter into the flow of life so that they understand their emotional sources, as well as how they can best use their time and energy to give back to society. They are dedicated to getting their grandchildren on track and to making sure that their families are balanced, but they also meet their own needs to give to those who are outside their families.

This orientation helps them to make sure that they continue to be forward looking in all their endeavors, and they show their grandchildren the grand scope of the possibilities and opportunities that await them.

Although special mission grandparents' ways of giving back to society need not involve grandiose plans or sweeping policies, they are guided by some ideals of progress when they decide what to do and which goals to pursue. Even though all a particular special grandparent may do is serve as an usher at a weekly religious service, this task is sufficiently outgoing to make a difference in the quality of life of that community. Thus contributions may indeed be small scale rather than broad ranging, and yet even these apparently minuscule actions will serve the purpose of linking grandparents, grandchildren, and families to the outside world and of giving back to society.

Duane and Theresa express their concerns and considerations about their families in a variety of ways, but as long as they cut themselves off from their communities, they will not be able to leave as enduring a legacy for their grandchildren as Nigel and Ginny. The outward-looking posture and actions of Nigel and Ginny help their grandchildren and their families to feel as though they belong to their community. This sense of belonging gives Nigel's and Ginny's family a greater sense of security and more opportunities for launching their members into useful roles in society.

Giving back to society therefore enriches the lives of grandparents, their grandchildren, and their families. Although it is accurate to say that special mission grandparents in entrenched traditional families, families in conflict, dysfunctional families, distant families, fragmented families, and blended families will not all be able to participate fully in giving back to society, because their energies may be largely drained by bringing their families into balance, special mission grandparents will ultimately head in this direction of giving back to society. What is particularly worrisome about Duane and Theresa is that in spite of having made many community contributions over the years, because of their professional expertise, they have chosen to move in a less productive direction in the long run. Even though attending to their family needs is a worthy goal, it is not sufficient of itself, given Duane's and Theresa's unrecognized needs to continue to give back to society.

Even getting reconnected with intergenerational processes in their families cannot relieve special mission grandparents of their ultimate responsibility to continue to give back to society. Getting to know the past better through compiling a family history is a means to an end, for example, rather than an end in itself. Special mission grandparents get to know their own heritage sufficiently so that they can create a legacy for others. Getting to know the details of one's generational connectedness is an empty exercise unless it is closely linked with activities that move in a direction of social progress.

GIVING BACK TO SOCIETY AND CHANGE

Special mission grandparents are deeply involved in change processes because they recognize that much needs to be changed in the world in order to improve the living situations of increased numbers of people. Therefore, giving back to society and accomplishing changes in the public interest are synonymous with each other for these grandparents. After first bringing about changes in their families, special mission grandparents move into broader arenas where they can pursue their own interests and exercise their own talents in accomplishing broad changes. Special mission grandparents are therefore opportunists in the sense that their goals to accomplish change might have to be put on hold until their timing and circumstances are propitious. When they see possibilities to be heard, or occasions to give, they move forward quickly to achieve their goals to change the status quo.

Special mission grandparents are sufficiently mature that they know what it takes to be heard, as well as what it takes to accomplish effective changes. Having weathered many pressures in their families, they are aware that the emotional quality of their contributions largely determines whether their initiatives are met with others' cooperation or resistance. They know that if they push too hard, or too dogmatically, for example, their efforts will be in vain. However, if they try to convince their audiences of the reasons or necessity for making a particular kind of change, they will be more likely to win their cooperation.

Ideally, special mission grandparents become historical actors through their efforts to give back to society. This means that they become sufficiently aware of what needs to be done in society at large and that they get actively engaged in directly accomplishing these goals. They know that their lives have a purpose that transcends their own limited life span, and they deliberately act in ways that connect their past, present, and future. Being a historical actor means that special mission grandparents go beyond their personal limitations and become heroic selves through making use of more of their potential.

Special mission grandparents also live out an ideal of staying busy with unfinished projects. There is no real retirement for these grandparents. Grandparents may discontinue their paid work, and thus be thought of by others as retired, but this is merely a conventional label for who they are. Special mission grandparents immediately engage in other interests and activities upon retirement from their paid work, especially in projects that help them to give back to society what they have gained themselves.

Special mission grandparents are particularly skilled in building on their personal and professional experiences of the past, so they can offer wisdom in solving current problems for a better future. In many respects it is this broad perspective through time that special mission grandparents bring to bear on the present and the future that is a basis of their health and a source of others' well-being. How these grandparents see change is therefore an invaluable contribution they can make to members of younger generations and to the wider society.

The contributions special mission grandparents make to their communities vary a great deal. They give back to society in ways that fit their own strengths and circumstances and that reflect their most cherished values. These end results of being a special mission grandparent do not mean that family changes are less important than giving back to society, but rather that all these ways of making contributions to society must be honored. Special mission grandparents recognize that it is a privilege to be alive so that giving to others is possible. They also know that making these kinds of contributions is truly empowering to them, their grandchildren, their relatives, and members of society.

Some of the ways in which special mission grandparents give back to society are listed below. They include the range of contributions made to their families as well as to society:

1. they balance and strengthen their families;
2. they protect their grandchildren from negative emotional influences in their families, and prevent or neutralize these tensions so that they no longer occur;
3. they create as many conditions as possible so that their grandsons and granddaughters will be treated equally in their families and in their communities;
4. they educate their grandchildren so that they will be compassionate in their dealings with others, as well as willing to give of themselves to those who are less fortunate than themselves;
5. they make their own unique contributions to their communities;
6. they become historical actors who transcend difficulties in their particular situations so that they can express their ideals in their actions;

7. they are examples to their grandchildren, their relatives, and members of society because of their heroic efforts to pursue their special missions;

8. they show their grandchildren how important it is to come full circle when they get older so that they can give back to society and improve life for others.

Because Duane and Theresa did not pursue these goals, they cannot be thought of as special mission grandparents. They are conscientious, conventional grandparents who gain a great deal of emotional satisfaction from their family and from making contributions to their family. It is also true that their grandchildren must benefit a great deal from their continuous care and attention.

On the other hand, Nigel and Ginny are model special mission grandparents because they are dedicated to both their families and their communities. They understand the importance of having secure, flexible family relationships, as well as the importance of continuing to make contributions to others, in order to give back to society. They have accomplished true maturity in that they know that their own future well-being is inextricably tied to the well-being of others in society, and they will not rest until social progress is attained for all.

It is this kind of broad dedication that makes Nigel and Ginny particularly effective grandparents. They have defined their special missions clearly and worked towards them effectively. They have also included their grandchildren in their activities sufficiently to give them a strong sense of belonging to their family and community. As a consequence, their grandchildren have learned that some day they too will find ways to give back to society and become special mission grandparents.

Suggested Reading

Beal, E. (1991). *The Adult Children of Divorce*. New York: Delacorte.

Boszormenyi-Nagy, I., and G. M. Spark (1973). *Invisible Loyalties*. New York: Harper.

Bott, Elizabeth (1957). *Family and Social Network*. London: Tavistock.

Bowen, Murray (1978). *Family Therapy in Clinical Practice*. New York: Jason Aronson.

Gilbert, Roberta M. (1992). *Extraordinary Relationships: A New Way of Thinking about Human Relationships*. Minneapolis: Chronimed.

Hall, C. Margaret (1991). *The Bowen Family Theory and Its Uses*. New York: Jason Aronson.

——— . (1998). *Heroic Self: Sociological Dimensions of Clinical Practice*. Springfield, IL: Charles C. Thomas.

——— . (1994). *New Families: Reviving and Creating Meaningful Bonds*. New York: Haworth.

Kerr, Michael, and Murray Bowen (1988). *Family Evaluation*. New York: W. W. Wiley.

Papero, D. V. (1990). *Bowen Family Systems Theory*. Boston: Allyn and Bacon.

Speck, R., and C. Attneave (1973). *Family Networks*. New York: Pantheon.

Toman, Walter (1993). *Family Constellation*. New York: Springer.

Turner, R. H. (1970). *Family Interaction*. New York: W. W. Wiley.

Young, M., and P. Willmott (1962). *Family and Kinship in East London*. Harmondsworth, Middlesex: Pelican.

Index

About the Author

C. MARGARET HALL is Professor of Sociology at Georgetown University, where she has also served as Department Chair and Director of Women's Studies. She has researched three-generation families for more than twenty-five years and has developed identity empowerment theory from her research and clinical data. Her publications include *Women and Empowerment: Strategies for Increasing Autonomy* (1992), *New Families: Reviving and Creating Meaningful Bonds* (1994), and *Identity, Religion, and Values: Implications for Practitioners* (1996).